Research into Practice

Implementing Effective Teaching Strategies

Alan Hofmeister

Margaret Lubke

Utah State University

Allyn and Bacon

Boston   London   Sydney   Toronto

Copyright © 1990 by Allyn and Bacon
A Division of Simon & Schuster, Inc.
160 Gould Street
Needham Heights, Massachusetts 02194

Library of Congress Cataloging-in-Publication Data
Hofmeister, Alan M.
   Research into practice : implementing effective teaching strategies / Alan Hofmeister and Margaret Lubke.
     p.   cm.
   Includes bibliographical references.
   ISBN 0-205-12290-6
   1. Teaching. 2. Education—Research. I. Lubke, Margaret.
II. Title.
LB1775.H56   1990
371.1′02—dc20
                                   89-37727
                                      CIP

Printed in the United States of America

10 9 8 7 6 5 4 3 2 1   93 92 91 90 89

CONTENTS

Preface   vii

Chapter 1   *Planning for Instructional Improvement*   1

     Towards a Frame of Reference   2
     "What Am I Doing for Students?"   3
     The Research Literature and the Implications   5
     The Purpose of This Book   7
     How to Use This Book   8
         Pre-service and In-service Use of This Book   9
         The First Step in Using This Book   10
     References   11

Chapter 2   *Time Management*   13

     A.   The Research Literature   14
         The "Active-direct" Teacher   14
         Time Management Concepts   15
     B.   Knowledge Quiz: Time Management   23
         Answer Key: Knowledge Quiz (Time Management)   26
     C.   Self-evaluation Checklist: Time Management   28
         Instructions for Completing the Self-evaluation
           Checklist   28
         Self-evaluation Checklist   30
     D.   Information Gathering: Assessing Engaged Time   32
         Defining Time-on-task Behaviors   32
         General Directions for Recording Time-on-task   32
         Assessing Transition Time   33
     E.   Practical Suggestions: Time Management   38
         Increasing Allocated Time   38
         Increasing Engaged Time   39
         Increasing Academic Learning Time   40
         Pacing Curriculum and Lessons   42
         Decreasing Transition Time   42
     F.   Self-improvement Plan: Time Management   45
     References   50

Chapter 3   Teaching Functions   **53**

    A. The Research Literature   54
        Teaching Function Concepts   55
        Getting It All Together to Meet Student Needs   62
    B. Knowledge Quiz: Teaching Functions   68
        Answer Key: Knowledge Quiz (Teaching Functions)   71
    C. Self-evaluation Checklist: Teaching Functions   73
        Instructions for Completing the Self-evaluation
          Checklist   74
        Self-evaluation Checklist   74
    D. Information Gathering: Teaching Functions   76
        Analyzing Instructional Presentations   76
        The Review Game   79
        Speaking Clearly and Fluently   82
    E. Practical Suggestions: Teaching Functions   84
        Daily, Weekly, and Monthly Reviews   84
        Presentation of New Content   84
        Guided Student Practice   86
        Independent Student Practice   87
    F. Self-improvement Plan: Teaching Functions   88
    References   91

Chapter 4   Academic Feedback   **93**

    A. The Research Literature   94
        Academic Feedback Concepts   95
        Academic Feedback and Independent Practice   100
        Expectations, Participation, and Feedback   104
    B. Knowledge Quiz: Academic Feedback   105
        Answer Key: Knowledge Quiz (Academic Feedback)   108
    C. Self-evaluation Checklist: Academic Feedback   110
        Instructions for Completing the Self-evaluation
          Checklist   110
        Self-evaluation Checklist   111
    D. Information Gathering: Academic Feedback   113
        Analyzing Questions   113
        Analyzing Feedback   117
    E. Practical Suggestions: Academic Feedback   120
        Question Types   120

	Delivering the Questions	121
	Reactions to Student Responses	122
F.	Self-improvement Plan: Academic Feedback	124
	References	127

Chapter 5 *Academic Monitoring*   129

A.	The Research Literature	130
	Academic Monitoring Concepts	131
B.	Knowledge Quiz: Academic Monitoring	140
	Answer Key: Knowledge Quiz (Academic Monitoring)	143
C.	Self-evaluation Checklist: Academic Monitoring	145
	Instructions for Completing the Self-evaluation Checklist	145
	Self-evaluation Checklist	146
D.	Information Gathering: Academic Monitoring	148
	The Academic Monitoring Form	148
	Interaction Monitoring	151
E.	Practical Suggestions: Academic Monitoring	154
	Monitoring and Goals	154
	Providing for Timely Monitoring	155
	Decision Making and Corrective Action	155
	Monitoring and the Improvement of Instruction	156
F.	Self-improvement Plan: Academic Monitoring	158
	References	160

Chapter 6 *Classroom Management*   161

A.	The Research Literature	162
	Management and Order	162
	Classroom Management Concepts	162
	Summary: Effective Classroom Management and the Profession	171
B.	Knowledge Quiz: Classroom Management	173
	Answer Key: Knowledge Quiz (Classroom Management)	176
C.	Self-evaluation Checklist: Classroom Management	178
	Instructions for Completing the Self-evaluation Checklist	178
	Self-evaluation Checklist	179

Contents

   D. Information Gathering: Classroom Management   181
       School Rules   181
       Daily Goals   184
   E. Practical Suggestions: Classroom Management   187
       Setting and Implementing Rules   187
       Managing Interventions   191
       Increasing Appropriate Behavior   191
   F. Self-improvement Plan: Classroom Management   193
   References   195

   Index   197

PREFACE

For the first time in the history of education, we have a body of research that addresses the essence of our profession, namely, the practices of our most effective teachers. Given that many educational research efforts have generated more speculation than valid practical applications, the consistency, generalizability, and applied nature of this body of research is welcome. The research demands the immediate attention of those concerned with the progressive and systematic improvement of the teaching profession.

This book focuses on instructional practices and student experiences that are consistently productive in the classrooms of our most effective teachers. For those often disappointed by what they perceived to be the "nondirective," "impractical," or "esoteric" nature of some educational research, the findings of this body of research on effective teaching provide practical direction and, it is hoped, appealing examples of the contributions of educational research.

Chapter 1 gives an overview of the subject and explains how the book can be used. To facilitate the classroom application of the research findings, each of the remaining chapters covers research findings in one area: time management (Chapter 2), teaching functions (Chapter 3), academic feedback (Chapter 4), academic monitoring (Chapter 5), and classroom management (Chapter 6). In the opening section of each of these chapters, the major practical implications of the research in the particular area are clarified and exemplified with reference to classroom practices and the supporting research. The second section consists of a quiz, with answers provided. Section C gives readers the self-evaluation tools to assess their present practices and the extent to which these practices are consistent with the recommendations of the research.

Once teachers have profiled their strengths, areas for improvement, and areas where they lack information, they can use the next two sections. Section D provides procedures for collecting objective information on teaching practices, and Section E lists practical suggestions for improving problem areas. The final section of each chapter is a set of procedures for implementing a continuous self-improvement process that consolidates strengths and replaces less effective practices with more effective ones.

This document has evolved through several versions and field-tests. We are particularly indebted to those teachers, principals, in-service trainers, and pre-service university instructors in Utah, Minnesota, South Carolina, Washington, and Wyoming who provided the feedback to improve each version and fuel our enthusiasm. Our special thanks to Judy Sozio, who demonstrated a special brand of professionalism as she suffered through three years of field-tests and revisions to prepare each version of the manuscript.

We have been heavily dependent on suggestions of users of previous versions of this document and would welcome additional suggestions. Such suggestions should be addressed to Alan Hofmeister at the College of Education, Utah State University, Logan, Utah, 84322-6800.

Alan Hofmeister
Margaret Lubke

CHAPTER 1

Planning
for Instructional Improvement

Towards a Frame of Reference

"What Am I Doing for Students?"

The Research Literature and the Implications

The Purpose of This Book

How to Use This Book

    Pre-service and In-service Use of This Book

    The First Step in Using This Book

References

Towards a Frame of Reference

The teacher in training and the experienced teacher are faced with a broad choice of alternative teaching practices. Many of the alternatives offer, at best, little more than a change. In some cases the alternative may simply be a faddish step backwards. It is clear that some teaching practices are ineffective—it is important to note that the practice (not the teacher) is ineffective. Teachers can change the impact they have on students through their selection of teaching practices.

One clear message of the research literature discussed in this book is that the teacher is the final arbiter of what happens in the classroom. Teacher supervisors, curriculum committees, and school boards may offer little more than general direction, regardless of assigned or assumed authority within the system. In the final analysis, the teacher determines what is taught and how it is taught.

Given that the teacher exercises considerable latitude over instruction, and that many of the available instructional alternatives are less effective than others, the teacher needs a frame of reference to discriminate among the instructional alternatives. It is the purpose of this book to provide part of that frame of reference.

The practices that the effective teaching literature identifies as having the greatest value are those that describe student learning experiences. For example, it is clear that effective teachers place a strong emphasis on achieving successful guided practice before moving to independent practice. The choice of instructional method is less important than the inclusion of a guided practice component in the teaching sequence. Thus, guided practice might be achieved by large-group instruction, the peer tutoring involved in cooperative learning, or well-integrated computer-assisted instruction.

A frame of reference to guide the selection of effective teaching practices should be practical in that it can be applied to a wide range of substantive daily problems. This frame of reference should be built on a consistent body of research. The effective teaching literature offers a base for an important part of this frame of reference. If the evolutionary pattern present in this body of research holds, future research findings can be expected to add to rather than contradict present knowledge.

"What Am I Doing for Students?"

One of the realities of the classroom is that resources are finite; decisions involve compromises in the allocation of resources, such as the teacher's time. These decisions will be easier if one places the primary emphasis on what happens to the student, deemphasizing some of the other characteristics of competing instructional practices. For example, although highly individualized instructional settings have considerable theoretical appeal to a number of educators, many small- and large-group settings are often very effective learning environments. However, regardless of the setting, situations are effective when teachers facilitate student engagement in learning tasks efficiently and provide rewarding social and personal experiences. The achievement of such student experiences is more important than fidelity to any particular instructional setting.

Teachers should never get trapped into trying to select instructional practices on the basis of such characteristics as group or individual instruction. It is necessary to see beyond these more visible trappings of an instructional practice, look to the student, and make decisions based on what happens to the student. Characteristics such as student engagement and student success must be given priority. Much of the research literature on effective teaching practices is based on the direct observation of students; it contains a wealth of information on student behavior as well as teacher behavior.

To some extent, the term *effective teaching literature* is misleading because it suggests a concern for just the relationships between teacher behavior and student outcomes. A more appropriate term might be *effective pupil learning experiences.* Researchers have pointed out that the literature addresses three components: (1) teacher performance, (2) pupil learning experiences, and (3) pupil outcomes (Medley, Soar, & Soar, 1975; Capie & Tobin, 1981). The component of pupil learning experiences is the central unit that links teacher behavior to pupil outcomes (see Figure 1.1).

One way in which the practical value of the effective teaching literature and of this book can be measured will be your ability to evaluate new teaching practices. If you have assimilated the lessons of the research literature, you should know what types of student learning experiences are needed to ensure the effectiveness of a teaching practice. The important question is not "What am I doing?" but "What am I doing to create learning experiences that result in positive student outcomes?"

FIGURE 1.1

The Focus of the Teacher Effectiveness Literature

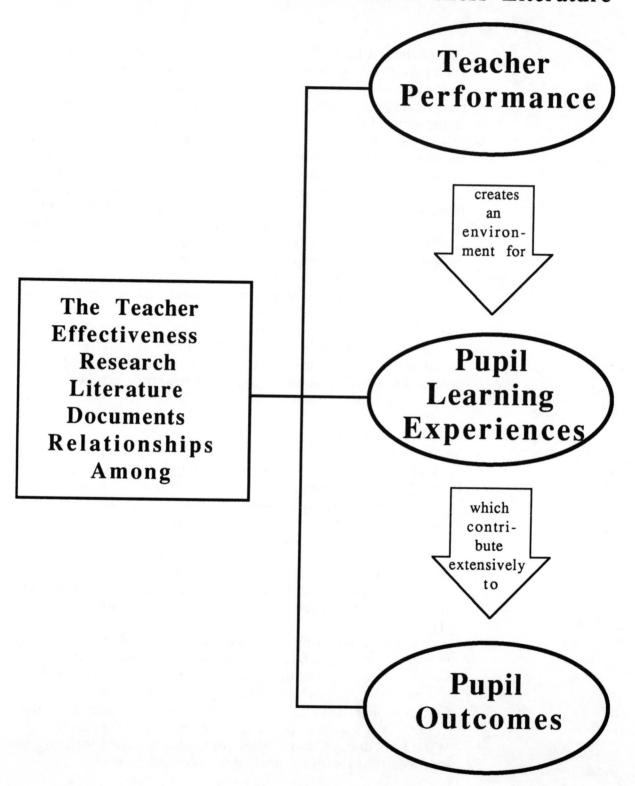

The Research Literature and the Implications

The past twenty years have seen the development and consolidation of the effective teaching literature. Earlier research findings suggested that the contributions of educators were comparatively ineffective when pitted against community and social forces. Recent analyses of the effective teaching literature affirm the importance of the teacher as a professional who can make a difference.

Most of the instructional skills identified in the effective teaching literature evolved through a two-stage process. The first stage was correlational. In this phase, researchers identified teaching practices that were consistently associated with the more effective teachers. The second stage was a validation stage, in which teachers were systematically trained in promising practices identified in earlier correlational studies. In summarizing one of these second-stage studies, Good, Grouws, and Ebmeier (1983) concluded,

> Our research provides compelling evidence that teachers make a difference in student learning and offers some useful information about how more and less effective teachers differ in their behavior and in their effects on student achievement [p. 13].

The effective teaching literature addresses attitudinal attributes, teaching skills, and student learning experiences that are consistently associated with effective teachers. In terms of attitude, the effective teacher is described as an individual confidently approaching teaching tasks with an expectation of success, a belief in the importance of teaching, and a sense of responsibility for the outcomes of the teaching process.

The teaching skills of the effective teacher are characterized by (1) a concern for the use of teacher and student time; (2) an emphasis on the curriculum; (3) the careful introduction of new material in small steps, integrated with guided practice and followed by carefully managed independent practice; (4) the careful monitoring of student progress, with coordinated reteaching; (5) attention to prerequisite skills and frequent reviewing to ensure that new content is successfully introduced and consolidated; and (6) a set of classroom management skills that involve a strong instructional program and active teacher involvement with all students in all phases of the instructional process.

In discussing the relative importance of the characteristics of effective instruction, Reynolds and Lakin (1987) made the following two observations. First, these are variables that can be altered by educators. Second, the value of these characteristics "that are associated with pupil achievement but that can be manipulated by educators, is greater than those over which educators have relatively little control (e.g., IQ, family background, class size)" (p. 338).

In a similar vein, Hunter (1984) made the following observation on the generalizability and importance of the findings from the effective teaching literature:

> Current findings are in direct contrast to the former fatalistic stance that regarded IQ and socioeconomic status as unalterable determinants of academic achievement. Gone also should be the notion that different ages, ethnic derivations, or content to be learned require a completely different set of professional skills, or that effective teachers must be born and can't be made. While the *form* may be different, the *substance* of excellence in teaching remains the same. Discoveries that dispelled these previously held educational myths are not entirely new, but recent translation from theory into teaching practice has effected the metamorphosis from a reactive to a proactive profession of education [p. 169].

The generalizability of the findings is, indeed, one of the most encouraging aspects of the effective teaching literature. Researchers have noted the consistency with which these effective teaching characteristics have been shown to be important in virtually all structured curriculum content areas, across elementary and high schools (Capie & Tobin, 1981; Rosenshine & Stevens, 1986), with regular classroom students, with preschool children (Lane & Bergan, 1988), and handicapped students (Bickel & Bickel, 1986; Gottlieb & Alter, 1984), and in Third World countries (Fuller, 1987).

Although the characteristics of effective teaching appear to be common denominators in a wide range of instructional settings, one should not assume that such characteristics make up the total act of teaching. A range of instructional activities can be added. For example, the effective instruction literature does not identify specific procedures for sequencing instruction or exemplifying concepts. Also, the effective teaching literature makes no detailed attempt to answer the question, "What do I teach?" The primary concern is, "How do I teach?"

All the answers may not be available, but what is available is both practical and important. Berliner (1984) stated,

> There are many variables recently uncovered in educational research that show as strong or stronger a relationship with student achievement and student behavior as variables in medical practice show to longevity and general health. But in medicine, such relationships become imperatives [for change], while in education they are treated as shreds—the merest glimmer of an implication [for change]. Our research is much less at fault than our attitudes towards research [p 75].

The Purpose of This Book

The central message of the effective instruction literature can be summarized as follows:

1. The effective instruction literature identifies teaching skills and student learning experiences that a teacher can use to increase instructional effectiveness.

2. There are undoubtedly other skills a teacher may add. These skills should be viewed as complements, not replacements, for the effective teaching skills.

3. Teaching skills vary greatly among teachers and are potent factors that teachers can modify so as to have a positive and substantive impact on students.

4. One measure of a professional is the extent to which he or she systematically uses relevant research findings to improve practice. The professional teacher has an obligation to engage in the following activities:

    a. Review the recommendations from the effective teaching literature

    b. Compare present classroom practices against the recommendations

    c. Implement changes

    d. Evaluate the extent to which the changes are consistent with the effective teaching literature

These four activities summarize the purpose of this book.

How to Use This Book

The different effective teaching variables and their implications for improving instruction are treated in Chapters 2 through 6, as follows:

Chapter 2: Time Management
Chapter 3: Teaching Functions
Chapter 4: Academic Feedback
Chapter 5: Academic Monitoring
Chapter 6: Classroom Management

Before publication in its present form, this book evolved through three field-test versions, which were used in both in-service and pre-service settings. The following suggestions for using the book came from observations made during the field-testing of the earlier versions.

Chapters 2 through 6 have similar structures, and each is divided into the following sections:

A. The Research Literature. In this section, the skills and concepts associated with the chapter topic are identified and discussed in relation to the research literature and their value as classroom practices.

B. Knowledge Quiz. This is a check for understanding of the material presented in Section A. Each Section B consists of a quiz and answers for the quiz.

C. Self-evaluation Checklist. This checklist allows teachers and student teachers to examine their present practices and determine the extent to which their classroom practices are consistent with the recommendations that follow from the research on effective teaching practices. In responding to each item on the checklist, the teacher may indicate that classroom practices are partially or wholly consistent, or the teacher might indicate a need to gather more information in that area.

D. Information Gathering. This section of each chapter consists of examples and suggestions of ways teachers may gather more objective information about classroom practices.

E. Practical Suggestions. In this section of each chapter, practical suggestions for typical problems are provided. These suggestions have been gleaned from numerous sources, including observations from the field-testing of earlier versions of this book and from the research literature.

F. Self-improvement Plan. Most master teachers did not become so overnight. Years of conscientious observations of the relationship between teacher actions, student experiences, and pupil behavior were used for progressive improvement of instructional practices. Over time, the less effective practices were replaced by more effective ones. This section of each chapter provides suggestions for this process of progressive improvement.

The central intent of the effective teaching research is the facilitation of professional growth through an objective view of history, rather than through a trial-and-error process that places students at considerable risk.

Pre-service and In-service Use of This Book

The book is structured to support both pre-service and in-service staff development activities. In the in-service field-testing of earlier versions, the book served as a guide to school principals and staffs working cooperatively over the whole school year to improve instruction progressively. Typically, planning meetings were held twice a month to discuss progress and plan future activities.

In pre-service settings or other situations in which participants do not have access to classrooms, the book can still make a major contribution. One of the most effective pre-service applications involves the following steps for each of Chapters 2 through 6:

Step 1. Participants review and discuss the material in Section A and then take the Section B knowledge quiz.

Step 2. Participants check their responses to the knowledge quiz and review any material not mastered.

Step 3. The instructor then provides participants with (real or simulated) completed self-evaluation checklists (see Section C). This will be most meaningful if participants can observe a classroom and complete their own checklists.

Step 4. Using these completed self-evaluation checklists, the participants, as individuals or small groups, prepare self-improvement plans (see Section F). The plans include procedures for improving instruction and for gathering more objective information. To develop the plans, the participants use the resources provided in Sections D and E of each chapter.

Step 5. Participants and instructor discuss and evaluate the self-improvement plans.

After reading Chapter 1, it is recommended, for both pre- and in-service applications, that you do a quick reading of Section A in each of Chapters 2 through 6 first, then return to Section A in Chapter 2, and proceed through the book in the traditional linear manner. Because the variables treated in the effective teaching literature are complex and interacting, a quick review of all variables will help the reader comprehend the nature of these relationships. This procedure also complements the intent of this chapter and supports one of the recommendations of the effective teaching literature: to clarify the direction of and the reason for the instruction before addressing the acquisition of new content in more detail.

References

Berliner, D. (1984). The half-full glass: A review of research on teaching. In P.L. Hosford (Ed.), *Using what we know about teaching* (pp. 51–77). Washington, D.C.: Association for Supervision and Curriculum Development.

Bickel, W.E., & Bickel, D.D. (1986). Effective schools, classrooms, and instruction: Implications for special education. *Exceptional Children, 52,* 489–500.

Capie, W., & Tobin, K.G. (1981). Pupil engagement in learning tasks: A fertile area for research in science teaching. *Journal of Research in Science Teaching, 18*(5), 409–417.

Fuller, B. (1987). What school factors raise achievement in the Third World? *Review of Educational Research, 57*(30), 255–292.

Good, T.L., Grouws, D.A., & Ebmeier, H. (1983). *Active mathematics teaching.* New York: Longman.

Gottlieb, J., & Alter, M. (1984). Perspectives on instruction. In E.L. Meyen (Ed.), *Mental retardation: Topics of today, issues of tomorrow* (CEC-MR monograph), *1*(1), 88–114.

Hunter, M. (1984). Knowing, teaching, and supervising. In P.L. Hosford (Ed.), *Using what we know about teaching* (pp. 169–195). Washington, D.C.: Association for Supervision and Curriculum Development.

Lane, S., & Bergan, J.R. (1988). Effects of instructional variables on language ability of preschool children. *American Educational Research Journal, 25*(2), 271–283.

Medley, D.M., Soar, R.S., & Soar, R. (1975). *Assessment and research in teacher education: Focus on PBTE.* Washington, D.C.: American Association of Colleges for Teacher Education.

Reynolds, M.C., & Lakin, K.C. (1987). Noncategorical special education: Models for research and practice. In M.C. Wang, M.C. Reynolds, & H.J. Walberg (Eds.), *Handbook of special education: Research and practice,* Vol. 1 (pp. 331–356). New York: Pergamon Press.

Rosenshine, B., & Stevens, R. (1986). Teaching functions. In M.C. Wittrock (Ed.), *AERA handbook of research on teaching,* 3rd ed., (pp. 376–391). New York: Macmillan.

CHAPTER 2

Time Management

A. The Research Literature
   The "Active-direct" Teacher
   Time Management Concepts
B. Knowledge Quiz: Time Management
   Answer Key: Knowledge Quiz (Time Management)
C. Self-evaluation Checklist: Time Management
   Instructions for Completing the Self-evaluation
      Checklist
   Self-evaluation Checklist
D. Information Gathering: Assessing Engaged Time
   Defining Time-on-task Behaviors
   General Directions for Recording Time-on-task
   Assessing Transition Time
E. Practical Suggestions: Time Management
   Increasing Allocated Time
   Increasing Engaged Time
   Increasing Academic Learning Time
   Pacing Curriculum and Lessons
   Decreasing Transition Time
F. Self-improvement Plan: Time Management
References

A. The Research Literature

In summarizing the findings from the research design to identify the characteristics of effective math teachers, Brophy (1986) made the following observation:

> . . . student achievement is maximized when teachers allocate most classroom time to activities designed to promote student achievement and use managerial and instructional strategies that support such achievement [p 3].

Without a doubt, the effective teacher ensures that students are appropriately engaged in instruction for as much of the available time as possible. Time is important. This is a consistent theme throughout the research, regardless of whether the findings are from studies comparing effective and ineffective teachers in the United States or from studies comparing the effectiveness of instruction in basic skills across different countries.

The "Active-direct" Teacher

A teacher's approach to the use of time is often tied to his or her assessment of a teacher's relative value in the classroom. If teachers feel that the time they spend with students has considerable value, they will work to increase the amount of time spent interacting with students.

The research on the characteristics of effective teachers has yielded a consistent profile of a teacher actively teaching, rather than depending on less direct approaches in which there is less instructional activity and less teacher contact with students. Brophy (1986), in reviewing the research on effective math instruction, reported that "Students achieve more in classes where they spend most of their time being taught or supervised by their teacher rather than working on their own or not working at all" (p. 4).

Borg (1980), in his summary of the research on the relationship between time and school learning, noted a consistent finding: "The amount of time that students are engaged in relevant reading and mathematics tasks is positively associated with academic achievement" (p. 59).

One of the major implications of the research on the effective use of time lies in the extent to which an individual teacher can manage the use of time. The research shows considerable variability among teachers teaching the same content at the same grade levels. Rosenshine (1980) noted that the teachers who were more successful at engaging students had their students engaged for two hours and thirty minutes per day, or 53 percent of the in-class time. The least successful teachers had students engaged for one hour and twenty minutes per day, or 28 percent of the in-class time. Berliner (1984) reported that some teachers generate very high engagement rates. He summed up the importance of student engagement with instruction tasks as follows:

> The fact that engaged time is so variable across classes is what is now well documented. There are classes where engagement rates are regularly under 50 percent, and those where engagement rates are regularly about 90 percent. One hour of allocated mathematics instruction, then, can result in either 30 minutes or 54 minutes of actual delivered instruction to students. In a single week, differences of such a magnitude can yield a difference of about two hours in the amount of mathematics that is actually engaged in by students. It is no wonder that in reading, mathematics or science, at any grade level, large variations in engaged time by students is a strong predictor of achievement [p. 57].

Time Management Concepts

Research on the effective use of time has generated several time management terms. The most common term is *time-on-task*, or *engaged time*. Other terms include *available time, allocated time, academic learning time* (or *ALT*), *pacing, transition time*, and *instructional momentum*. (See Figure 2.1.)

1. Available Time. This is the time available for all school activities. The available time is limited by the number of days in a school year (approximately 180 days) and the number of hours in a school day (approximately six hours, including one hour of break time). Available time will be divided among all the diverse functions of a school, including the recreational, social, and academic goals that form the mandated and the hidden curriculum present in every school district.

Schools vary only slightly in the number of school days in a school year, but there is considerably more variability in the hours assigned per day and in the average daily attendance. Variations of up to two hours per day among school districts have been noted (Stallings, 1975). The data on average daily attendance has shown that some schools within the same district provided 50 percent more schooling than other schools because of variations in average daily attendance (Wiley & Harnischfeger, 1974).

2. Allocated Time. Allocated time is the amount of time assigned for instruction in a content area, without reference to the quality of the activities being conducted during that time. In allocating time to a specific curriculum area, one must consider how the time

FIGURE 2.1

Time and the School Day

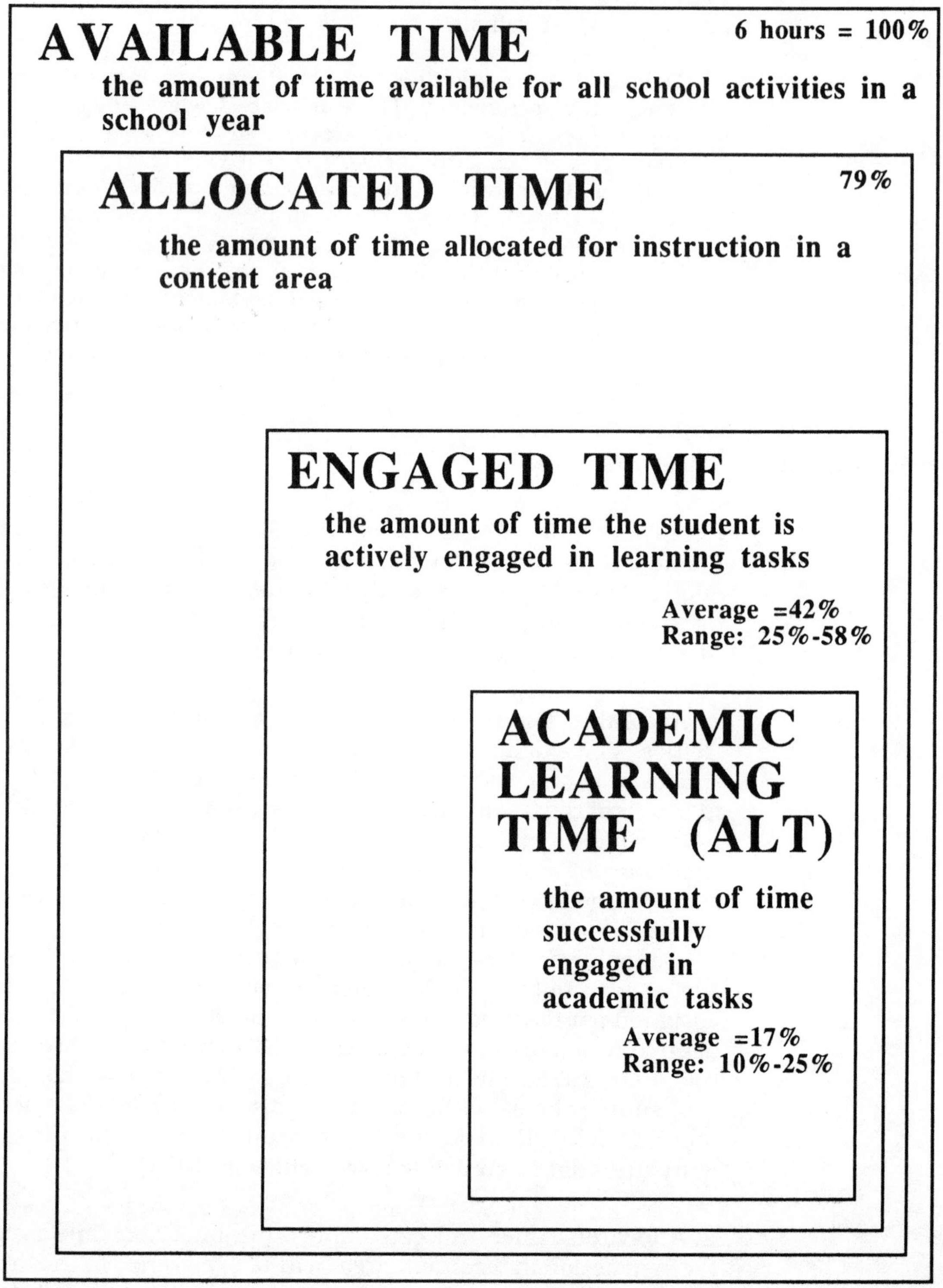

AVAILABLE TIME
6 hours = 100%

the amount of time available for all school activities in a school year

ALLOCATED TIME
79%

the amount of time allocated for instruction in a content area

ENGAGED TIME

the amount of time the student is actively engaged in learning tasks

Average =42%
Range: 25%-58%

ACADEMIC LEARNING TIME (ALT)

the amount of time successfully engaged in academic tasks

Average =17%
Range: 10%-25%

is allocated as well as total time set aside for the class. The amount of time and the way it is distributed during the day, week, and school year are issues related to allocated time. In an extensive multiyear study of teaching practices, the following findings on the allocation of time were reported (Fisher et al., 1980):

> Within reading and mathematics, classes differed in the amount of time allocated to different skill areas. For example, in one second-grade class, the average student received 9 minutes of instruction over the whole school year in the arithmetic associated with the use of money. This figure can be contrasted with classes where the average second grader was allocated 315 minutes per school year in the curriculum content area of money. As another example, in the fifth grade some classes received less than 1,000 minutes of instruction in reading comprehension for the second year (about 10 minutes per day). This figure can be contrasted with classes where the average student was allocated almost 5,000 minutes of instruction related to comprehension during the school year (about 50 minutes per day) [p. 16].

Berliner (1984), in a review of the research literature on content decision, made the following observations:

- The assumption that the curriculum and associated time allocations are set by school boards and administrators is only partly true. The final arbiter of what is taught is the classroom teacher.
- The research has documented wide variations among teachers for both content and time allocation decisions, even in the presence of clear and mandatory regulations detailing content and time allocations.
- The empirical data relating content coverage, or content emphasis to achievement, is clear. The opportunity to learn a content area is perhaps the most potent variable in accounting for achievement in that area.

Berliner concluded his review of content decision with the following statement by Buchmann and Schmidt (1981):

> During the school day, elementary school teachers can be a law unto themselves, favoring certain subjects at their discretion. What is taught matters, hence arbitrariness in content decisions is clearly inappropriate. If personal feelings about teaching subject matters are not bounded by an impersonal conception of professional duties, children will suffer the consequences. Responsibility in content decision making requires that teachers examine their own conduct, its main springs and potential effects on what is taught [p. 54].

3. Engaged Time. Engaged time is the amount of time the student is actively involved in such learning tasks as writing, listening, and responding to teacher questions. Engaged time does not include classroom tasks such as handing in a paper or waiting for a teacher to pass out materials, or inappropriate activities such as disruptive talking to another student or daydreaming.

Doyle (1986), in reporting on some of the most well-documented research on teacher behavior by Gump (1967), stated:

> Gump found that approximately one-half of the teachers' acts involved instruction (questions, feedback, imparting knowledge, etc.). The rest of the time the teachers were involved in organizing and arranging students for instruction and orienting them to tasks (23% average), dealing with deviant behavior (14%), and handling individual problems and social amenities (12%) [p. 399].

4. Academic Learning Time (ALT). Academic learning time has been defined as time spent by a student engaged on a task in which few errors are produced and where the task is directly relevant to an academic outcome (Romberg, 1980). The concept of ALT represents a considerable refinement over engaged time. Romberg noted that ALT is positively correlated with achievement, whereas time unsuccessfully engaged in academic tasks is negatively related to student achievement.

In order to determine which tasks were *directly* relevant to an academic outcome, ALT researchers emphasized correspondence between the tasks and the tests that would be used to measure student achievement. The alignment among the teacher's instruction, student learning activities, the curriculum, and tests of student outcomes is an important issue that will be treated in more detail in Chapter 5. ALT addresses one of these relationships—namely, the alignment between the student learning activity and the test used to measure student outcomes. Clearly, increasing academic learning time is a high priority for the teacher. The measurement of ALT is complex, because one has to combine the assessment of the time-on-task with measures of success and measures of the appropriateness of the learning tasks.

In one study (Fisher et al., 1980) that documented ALT in a large number of classrooms, it was noted that ALT varied from four to fifty-two minutes per day. The researchers commented on this finding as follows:

> It may appear that this range from 4 to 52 minutes per day is unrealistically large. However, these times actually occurred in the classes in the study. Furthermore, it is easy to imagine how either 4 or 52 minutes per day of Academic Learning Time might come about. If 50 minutes of reading instruction per day is allocated to a student who pays attention about a third of the time, and one-fourth of the student's reading time is at a high level of success, the student will experience only about 4 minutes of engaged reading at a high success level. Similarly, if 100 minutes per day is allocated to reading for a student who pays attention 85 percent of the time at a high level of success for almost two-thirds of the time, [he or she] will experience about 52 minutes of Academic Learning Time per day [p. 23].

The ALT notion of success in the engaged tasks represents a major refinement of the concept of engaged time. Marliave and Filby (1985) noted that "student success during instructional tasks is an ongoing learning behavior of equal or greater importance than that of time allocated to criterion-relevant tasks or student attention during those tasks" (p. 222).

5. Pacing. Pacing has two related dimensions. One dimension, curriculum pacing, is concerned with the rate at which progress is made through the curriculum. The second dimension, lesson pacing, is concerned with the pace at which a teacher conducts individual lessons. One team of researchers summed up the importance of pacing as follows:

> . . . researchers have shown that most students, including low-achieving students, learn more when their lessons are conducted at a brisk pace, because a reasonably fast pace serves to stimulate student attentiveness and participation, and because more content gets covered by students. This assumes, of course, that the lesson is at a level of difficulty that permits a high rate of student success; material that is too difficult or presented poorly cannot be learned at any instructional pace [Wyne, Stuck, White, & Coop, 1986, p. 20].

Berliner (1984), in discussing the rate at which progress is made through the curriculum, reported:

> The evidence for the power of the pacing variable keeps mounting. The more the teacher covers, the more students seem to learn. This is hardly shocking news. But again, it is the variability across classes that is most impressive. One teacher adjusts the pace in the workplace and covers half the text in a semester; another finishes it all. One teacher has 20 practice problems covered in a lesson, another manages to cover only 10. One teacher has students who develop a sight vocabulary of 100 words before Christmas, another teacher's students learn only 50 [p. 55].

Thus pacing, like many other characteristics of effective instruction, shows considerable variability among teachers and has a pronounced effect on student achievement.

In comparing the effective and less effective teachers, Good, Grouws, and Ebmeier (1983) noted that the less effective teachers covered 37 percent less when measured on a daily rate. Less effective teachers tended to try and catch up late in the course and then provided too much material without any distributed practice to consolidate and review the content. Clearly, the amount of content covered daily relates to other skills and should be viewed as both a symptom and a cause.

6. Transition Time. A lesson consists of a series of related instructional activities, including demonstrations, discussions, guided practice, and independent practice. Considerable time can be wasted if the transitions between these different activities within a lesson are not managed quickly and smoothly. To facilitate smooth transitions that maintain instructional momentum and student attention, teachers must demonstrate a wide range of curriculum and classroom management skills.

One method of reducing transition time (which is not necessarily recommended) involves reducing the number of lesson activities. For example, a teacher who confines a lesson to one activity ("Work the examples at the end of Chapter 6 and raise your hand if you want help") will have no trouble with transition time, because transitions will be eliminated. However, the omission of activities, such as guided practice, may reduce learning outcomes.

For transitions to occur quickly and smoothly,

- The teacher must have materials ready and demonstrate confidence in closing one activity and initiating the next.
- The teacher must exercise increased vigilance during the transition period.
- The student must enter the next activity with interest and the expectation of success.

In summarizing the research on effective instruction and transitions, Doyle (1986) made the following observation:

> . . . skilled managers marked the onset of transitions clearly, orchestrated transitions actively, and minimized the loss of momentum during these changes in activities. Less effective managers, on the other hand, tended to blend activities together, failed to monitor events during transitions, and took excessively long to complete the movement between segments. Transitions appear to require considerable vigilance and teacher direction to accomplish successfully [p. 416].

The skillful management of transitions does far more than save time. Kounin and Doyle (1975) reported that misbehavior is most likely to occur when there is a lag in the continuity of a lesson. Gump (1967) found that teachers dealt with more deviant behaviors during transitions than during any other time. Ross (1983) stated that the management of transitions was one of the most critical management tasks faced by teachers. No surgeon manipulates more interacting complex variables in a short time span than does the master teacher managing a transition. Ross (1983) searched the research literature for management procedures for "reducing the chaos of transitions" and identified a number of principles, including advance preparation, use of routines, and movement management. These principles are discussed in more detail in Section E of this chapter.

7. Instructional Momentum. Pacing and transition time management contribute to instructional momentum (see Figure 2.2).

FIGURE 2.2

INSTRUCTIONAL MOMENTUM

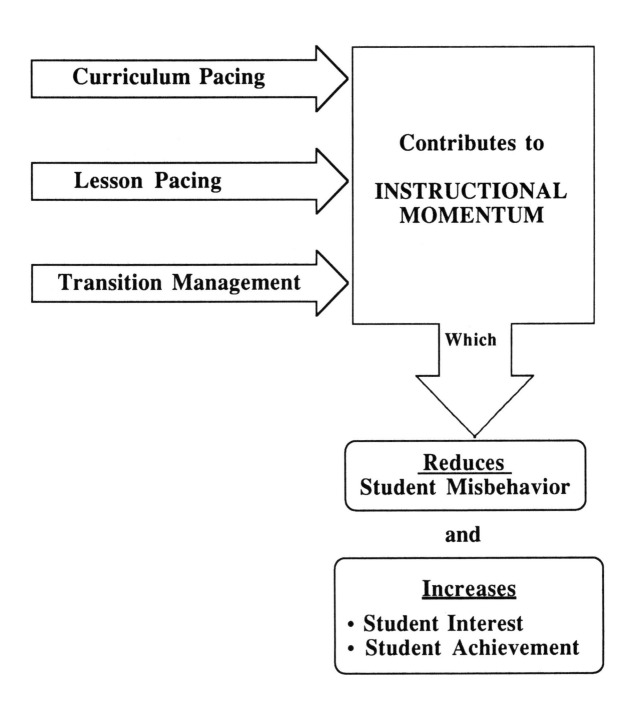

Both teacher and student need to feel a sense of movement through the curriculum. A loss of momentum will indicate structural problems in the instruction. A prolonged loss of momentum will have destructive, affective consequences for both teacher and student, as well as a negative effect on student achievement. Fortunately, the reverse of this is also true. Well-maintained momentum has positive affective consequences for student and teacher.

B. Knowledge Quiz: Time Management

Multiple Choice

Question 1

a. *Allocated time* refers to the quality and quantity of time available.

b. *Allocated time* refers to the quantity of time available for instruction.

c. There is little relationship between allocated time and student achievement.

d. There is no relationship between allocated time and student achievement.

Question 2

a. Engaged time includes the time a student spends waiting quietly for the lesson start.

b. Helping the teacher set up the overhead projector is engaged time.

c. Time spent on "busy work" is not engaged time.

d. Time spent actively engaged in all instructional tasks is engaged time.

Question 3

a. ALT is essentially the same as engaged time.

b. ALT is academic looking time.

c. ALT places an emphasis on student success in the task.

d. Increasing the number of transitions increases ALT.

Question 4

a. Learning is increased if each lesson is restricted to a single learning activity, such as guided practice or independent practice.

b. The time spent in changing from teacher demonstration to student practice would be an example of transition time.

c. Increasing transition time increases achievement, because teachers and students can get a much needed rest.

d. Reducing the number of lesson activities reduces transition time and increases achievement.

Question 5

a. Slowing the presentation pace is the best way to help low achievers.

b. Allowing students to work independently at their own pace is clearly the only way to go.

c. *Pacing* refers to both the rate at which the class progresses through the curriculum and the pace at which lessons are conducted.

d. A brisk pace should always be used, regardless of student success.

Question 6 An engaged time level of 90 percent

a. is impossible.

b. can be accomplished regularly by very effective teachers.

c. is typical of most teachers.

d. is easily achieved.

Question 7 In schools where the curriculum content and time allocations are clear,

a. there is little variability in engaged time among teachers.

b. there is virtually no variability in engaged time.

c. there will be only modest variability in engaged time, based on student needs.

d. time allocations can vary by several hundred percent.

Question 8 Research shows that the final arbiter of what is taught is

a. the teacher.

b. the curriculum supervisor.

c. the superintendent.

d. the school board.

Question 9 Research shows that, provided teachers use the same text,

a. there is little difference in the amount of material covered.

b. there can be a large difference in material covered.

c. there is little variability in what students learn.

d. difference in content covered will be related to student needs.

Question 10 Effective transitions

a. provide a break for the teacher.

b. give students a lengthy break.

c. require increased vigilance by the teacher.

d. take the pressure off teacher and students.

Fill in the Blanks

Question 11   The approximate time allocations in a school day are 100 percent for available time,

a. 79 percent for _____

b. 42 percent for _____

c. 17 percent for _____

Question 12

a. _____

b. _____, and

c. _____ contribute to instructional momentum.

Question 13   The majority of behavior problems occur during _____.

Question 14   _____ refers to the amount of time allocated for instruction in a content area.

Question 15   The notion of student success is a part of _____ _____, but is not present in engaged time.

Answer Key: Knowledge Quiz (Time Management)

Multiple Choice

Question 1

b. *Allocated time* refers to the quantity of time available for instruction.

Question 2

d. Time spent actively engaged in all instructional tasks is engaged time.

Question 3

c. ALT places an emphasis on student success in the task.

Question 4

b. The time spent in changing from teacher demonstration to student practice would be an example of transition time.

Question 5

c. *Pacing* refers to both the rate which the class progresses through the curriculum and the pace at which lessons are conducted.

Question 6   An engaged time level of 90 percent

b. can be accomplished regularly by very effective teachers.

Question 7   In schools where the curriculum content and time allocations are clear,

d. time allocation can vary by several hundred percent.

Question 8   Research shows that the final arbiter of what is taught is

a. the teacher.

Question 9   Research shows that, provided the teachers use the same text,

b. there can be a large difference in material covered.

Question 10   Effective transitions

c. require increased vigilance by the teacher.

Fill in the Blanks

Question 11   The approximate time allocations in a school day are 100 percent for available time,

a. 79 percent for *allocated time*

b. 42 percent for *engaged time*

c. 17 percent for *academic learning time*

Question 12

a. *Curriculum pacing,*

b. *lesson pacing,* and

c. *transition management* contribute to instructional momentum.

Question 13

The majority of behavior problems occur during *transitions.*

Question 14

Allocated time refers to the amount of time allocated for instruction in a content area.

Question 15

The notion of student success is a part of *ALT*, but is not present in engaged time.

C. Self-evaluation Checklist: Time Management

Instructions for Completing the Self-evaluation Checklist

A self-evaluation checklist is provided in Chapters 2 through 6, covering the following five areas, respectively:

Chapter 2: Time Management
Chapter 3: Teaching Functions
Chapter 4: Academic Feedback
Chapter 5: Academic Monitoring
Chapter 6: Classroom Management

Each of the checklists evaluates five major instructional skills. For example, Skill 2 on the Time Management Checklist addresses engaged time, and the instructional skill is broadly defined by the statement, "A high percentage of the allocated time is spent 'on-task' by students." Several evaluation questions are provided in each skill area. These evaluation questions provide a functional definition of the instructional skills and a vehicle for the self-evaluation process. You should feel free to add additional evaluation questions that further describe your instructional practices in this area.

For each evaluation question, you should fill in a numerical rating and any helpful comments that will further describe the skill. For the numerical rating, use the following four-point scale and associated criteria.

1 = No change is needed in present practices.
2 = There are minor problems that can be corrected quickly and easily.
3 = There are major problems that will require a considerable investment in time and effort.
4 = I need more specific information on my own behavior before I can decide whether I have a problem.

In most cases, the numbers 2 through 4 should be followed by a comment that addresses the issue in more detail. It will be helpful in the subsequent planning for instructional improvement if the comment addresses the context. For example, the evaluation question, "a. Does a lesson start quickly and smoothly?" might be followed by a rating of "2," indicating a minor problem. This rating might then be followed by the comment, "Have difficulty with Monday morning language arts lessons." Such a comment would not be unusual for a teacher who makes a considerable investment in class preparation on weekdays but might not be highly prepared on Mondays.

If the teacher had difficulty achieving a smooth, quick start to most of the daily language arts lessons, a rating of "3," indicating a major problem, would be more appropriate. Any ineffective instructional practice that is consistently present, or any practice that adversely and systematically affects the quality of education of even one student, should be classified as a major problem.

Please feel free to make photocopies of the self-evaluation checklists. The copyright on the self-evaluation checklists is waived in cases where the copies are used in conjunction with this book.

You will notice that no attempt has been made to provide global numerical scores. The book is intended to facilitate instructional improvement rather than the classification of teachers based on some number. The intent of the evaluation effort will be achieved by a progressive and systematic process that consolidates strengths and replaces less effective instructional practices with more effective ones. Any attempt to summarize or provide global numerical scores might serve only to deemphasize the specific practical information needed to drive the self-improvement process.

A professional evaluation effort is not something that occurs once every year or two and culminates in some global classification of a teacher; it should involve the teacher in an active and continuous role. Teachers should accept the primary responsibility for identifying practices that consolidate strengths and replace less effective practices with more effective ones. In Section F of this chapter, you will find suggestions for the self-improvement planning process.

Self-evaluation Checklist

Skill 1. Allocated Time
The maximum possible time is allocated for direct intensive instruction.

Evaluation Questions	Rating and Notes	
a. Are the time allocations for class changes and breaks unnecessarily long?		
b. Are non-curricular activities taking time that could be allocated to curricular activities?		
c. Do the time allocations reflect teacher interests rather than student needs?		
d. Is allocated time scheduled to ensure that continuity and systematic review are facilitated?		

Skill 2. Engaged Time
A high percentage of allocated time is spent "on-task" by students.

Evaluation Questions	Rating and Notes	
a. Does the lesson start quickly and smoothly?		
b. How long after the start of a lesson did it take to have all students on-task?		
c. Are large amounts of the allocated time being taken up with managerial tasks?		
d. Is transition time for lesson activities excessive?		
e. Is there a reduction in instructional intensity near the end of a lesson?		

Rating Scale: 1 - No change; 2 - Minor problems; 3 - Major problems; 4 - Insufficient information

Skill 3. Individual Engaged Time
All students, low and high achievers, are on-task.

Evaluation Questions	Rating and Notes	
a. Is the teacher moving about the classroom, actively checking on all students?		
b. Do the teacher's questioning procedures suggest a preference for high or low achievers?		
c. Does the teacher structure activities so that student non-participation is facilitated?		
d. Are the high achieving students becoming bored?		
e. Are attractive "back-up" activities available for early finishers?		

Skill 4. Teacher Use of Time
Teacher practices model a concern for the effective use of instructional time.

Evaluation Questions	Rating and Notes	
a. Are all instructional materials and equipment available and operational at the start of the lesson?		
b. Is the teacher physically in the room at the start of the lesson?		
c. Have assignments been corrected in a timely manner?		
d. Is the teacher giving full attention to the instructional tasks?		
e. Is the teacher conducting the lesson at a brisk and interesting pace?		

Skill 5. Academic Learning Time
Indicators of academic learning time (ALT) should provide evidence of progressive improvement in instruction.

Evaluation Questions	Rating and Notes	
a. Are high, average, and low achievers on-task and successful?		
b. Am I aware of the amount of "on-task" behavior of all individuals in my class?		
c. Am I aware of the actual levels of mastery of individuals in my class?		
d. Has individual "on-task" and mastery information been combined to profile instructional strengths and weaknesses?		
e. Is information on ALT directing efforts to improve instruction?		

D. Information Gathering: Assessing Engaged Time

Collecting information on engaged time requires careful attention to both logistics and measurement. Students and teachers often feel uncomfortable when observers record information about what happens in their classrooms. If you attempt to use one of these two formats, try to be as unobtrusive as possible. If you wish to record information about your own students, it will be easiest if you have another person teach while you do the recording. However, you may be able to use either of the two procedures during a seatwork session or similar type of activity.

Defining Time-on-task Behaviors

Time-on-task behaviors and attending behaviors are regarded here as being synonymous, defined as follows. The student is on-task/attending when exhibiting the following behaviors:

a. Looking at the assigned task

b. Appropriately applying tools (pencil, calculator, crayon, scissors, etc.) to the completion of the task

c. Manipulating objects essential to the task (typing on the keyboard of a typewriter or computer, throwing/catching a ball, etc.)

d. Responding verbally to a question

e. Raising a hand for attention to participate in the task

f. Exhibiting facial expressions that suggest a thoughtful contemplation of the task

g. Participating as an active member of a group engaged in a problem-solving activity

h. Any other behavior that appears to be clearly in line with what has been assigned (Latham, 1985)

General Directions for Recording Time-on-task

a. Position yourself so that you have a clear view of the student(s).

b. Be as unobtrusive as possible, keeping pencils, paper, and other recording tools out of sight, if possible.

c. Avoid eye contact with the student(s).

d. Using Form 2.1b, fill in the spaces at the top of the page.

e. During the first second of each one-minute interval, observe the student. Use the sweephand on a clock, wristwatch, or stopwatch to help keep track of intervals.

f. Write the number from the checklist that best matches the student's behavior, and then circle "yes" to signify on-task or "no" to signify off-task. (See the completed sample, Form 2.1a) *Do not* change your notation if the behavior changes after the first second of the interval. Your first notation must stand (unless, of course, you simply made a recording error). Randomness will tend to assure equality: Whereas in one instance, a student may be observed not to be engaged at the moment of the recording but then to return immediately to task, the opposite is as likely to occur during a subsequent interval.

g. To compute the percentage of engaged behavior for the observation period, divide the number of cells containing a "yes" by the total number of cells.

Assessing Transition Time

Collecting information on transition time can be accomplished by recording the time of day the transition occurs, the type of transition (between activities or within activities), and the length (in minutes and seconds) of the transition period. Please refer to the completed sample (Form 2.2a) for specifics on how to use the blank Transitions form (Form 2.2b).

Time On-Task

School _Hillcrest_   Date _December 14, 1988_

Student _Lynnette_   Observer _Toni C._

	Activity _Reading_	Scheduled Start Time _9:00 A.M._
		Actual Start Time _9:04 A.M._

Minutes	Scheduled Start Time 9:00 A.M.	On-task (yes) or Off-task (no)	Student Behavior (See Checklist below)
1	minute	Yes (No)	1
2	minutes	Yes (No)	4
3	minutes	Yes (No)	4
4	minutes	Yes (No)	2
5	minutes	(Yes) No	1
6	minutes	(Yes) No	4
7	minutes	(Yes) No	5
8	minutes	Yes (No)	5
9	minutes	(Yes) No	1
10	minutes	(Yes) No	6
11	minutes	Yes (No)	4
12	minutes	Yes (No)	6
13	minutes	(Yes) No	2
14	minutes	(Yes) No	2
15	minutes	(Yes) No	3

Checklist

Yes

1. Looking at the assigned task
2. Appropriately applying tools (pencil, calculator, crayon, scissors, etc.)
3. Manipulating objects essential to the task (typing, etc.)
4. Responding verbally to questions
5. Raising hand for attention to participate
6. Participating as an active member in a group activity (oriented toward group)

No

1. Looking around the room
2. Inappropriately applying tools (pencil, calculator, crayon, scissors, etc.)
3. Manipulating objects that are not essential to the task
4. Talking to neighbor, making inappropriate sounds
5. Calling out
6. Oriented away from the group or seated outside the group

Time On-Task

School _____   Date _____

Student _____   Observer _____

Activity _____	Scheduled Start Time _____ Actual Start Time _____	
Minutes	**Scheduled Start Time** _____	**On-task (yes) or Off-task (no)**	**Student Behavior (See Checklist below)**
1	minute	Yes No	
2	minutes	Yes No	
3	minutes	Yes No	
4	minutes	Yes No	
5	minutes	Yes No	
6	minutes	Yes No	
7	minutes	Yes No	
8	minutes	Yes No	
9	minutes	Yes No	
10	minutes	Yes No	
11	minutes	Yes No	
12	minutes	Yes No	
13	minutes	Yes No	
14	minutes	Yes No	
15	minutes	Yes No	

Checklist

Yes

1. Looking at the assigned task
2. Appropriately applying tools (pencil, calculator, crayon, scissors, etc.)
3. Manipulating objects essential to the task (typing, etc.)
4. Responding verbally to questions
5. Raising hand for attention to participate
6. Participating as an active member in a group activity (oriented toward group)

No

1. Looking around the room
2. Inappropriately applying tools (pencil, calculator, crayon, scissors, etc.)
3. Manipulating objects that are not essential to the task
4. Talking to neighbor, making inappropriate sounds
5. Calling out
6. Oriented away from the group or seated outside the group

TRANSITIONS

School _Adams_   Date _3/3/89_

Teacher _Mr. Allred_   Observer _Sheila H._

| Time of Day | Description of Transition | | | Length of Transition |
| | Between Activities | | Within Activities | |
	From	To	(Describe)	
8:10		→	Passing out math sheets	45 sec.
8:30	Math	→ Reading		2 min.
9:00		→	Lining up for recess	1' 30 sec.
9:15	Recess	→ Music		3 min.
		→		
		→		
		→		
		→		
		→		
		→		
		→		
		→		
		→		
		→		
		→		
		→		
		→		
		→		
		→		
		→		

TRANSITIONS

School _____ **Date** _____

Teacher _____ **Observer** _____

Time of Day	Description of Transition			Length of Transition
	Between Activities		Within Activities	
	From	To	(Describe)	
	→			
	→			
	→			
	→			
	→			
	→			
	→			
	→			
	→			
	→			
	→			
	→			
	→			
	→			
	→			
	→			
	→			

E. Practical Suggestions: Time Management

The practical suggestions in this section represent a collection of ideas based on classroom observations, experience, and a review of the effective teaching literature and teacher magazines. Feel free to incorporate any of these suggestions that work for you.

Increasing Allocated Time

a. Keep Sufficient Materials and Supplies Available.
  (1) Run off extra worksheets. Use them with students who "forget" their homework assignments.
  (2) Have worksheets/activities planned for students who finish early.
  (3) Make certain worksheets are sequenced in the order they will be used.
  (4) If there is more than one page in a handout, be sure that you have collated and stapled the pages.
  (5) Elicit the assistance of students or parent volunteers in completing preparation activities.
b. Have Necessary Equipment and Supplies Available.
  (1) If you are using audio equipment, test the equipment before you plan to use it.
  (2) If you are using a film projector or an overhead projector, make certain you have a spare bulb available.
  (3) Make certain you have sufficient extension cords and electrical adapters.
  (4) Check to see if a technical person will be available when you plan to use audiovisual equipment. Know where to find this person.
  (5) Regularly check to see that you have sufficient supplies of office materials such as pens, pencils, and markers.
c. Keep Materials and Equipment Easily Accessible.
  (1) Store materials near the area where they are to be used. Transportable boxes may be helpful.
  (2) Use file folders to store worksheets for separate individuals or groups.
  (3) Keep your daily schedule and lesson plans open on your desk or worktable.

d. Plan the Collection and Correction of Homework.

    (1) Ask students who have not finished their homework to write "yes" on the blackboard. (You can then easily count how many students have finished their homework and how many have not.)

    (2) When calling roll, have students respond "yes" if they have done their homework, and "no" if they have not.

    (3) Ask for choral answers to each problem in a homework assignment. When the chorus weakens, tag the problem as being difficult. As each answer is given, ask students to circle the problems they have worked incorrectly.

    (4) Count the number of students who answered each problem correctly and incorrectly by calling out the problem number and asking students to raise their hands if they answered the problem correctly.

    (5) If a student fails to return a homework assignment, have him or her take a duplicate copy of the assignment and begin working on it in another part of the classroom. Reinforce the student for working quietly.

    (6) If a student has partially completed a homework assignment, ask him or her to correct as much of it as is completed and then proceed to another part of the room to complete the work. Reinforce the student for working quietly.

The entire homework-checking procedure should take less than five minutes.

Increasing Engaged Time

a. Begin Classwork on Schedule.

    (1) Establish a schedule of classes and post a copy where all students can see it.

    (2) Initially, provide a reward for those who begin classwork on schedule. Gradually tone down the reward and praise for those who begin on time.

b. Get the Attention of the Class.

    (1) Give a signal or verbal prompt, such as "When everyone is sitting quietly, we will begin our math lesson."

    (2) Wait until all students have come to order before beginning the class.

    (3) Praise the group when all students are attending.

c. Get the Class Started after Breaks in the Schedule.

    (1) Establish a routine activity, such as a three-minute math facts sheet, to begin immediately after a break. During the break, place math facts worksheets face down on students' desks.

      (2) Use the setting of a kitchen timer as the signal to begin work.

      (3) Develop a set of index cards with review questions. Begin the class by randomly selecting two or three of the questions and asking the group to answer them. "Brain teasers" or riddles may also be used in a similar manner.

d. Use Nondisruptive Signals to Get Students Involved.

      (1) Use eye contact to indicate desired behavior.

      (2) Use a hand signal to designate appropriate behavior.

      (3) Post room rules in the classroom. Use a verbal cue, such as "Remember what *to* do," to indicate that students should refer to the appropriate rule.

      (4) Stand near those students who might have difficulty focusing on their work.

e. Focus Students' Attention on Instructional Tasks.

      (1) Use a verbal prompt such as, "Ready!"

      (2) Inform students of a reinforcing activity that is contingent on completing a particular task. For example, say, "When we have finished this math worksheet, it will be time for recess."

f. Circulate around the Room.

      (1) First, make certain that the work has been well prepared, introduced, and explained, so that most students can progress smoothly through an independent practice assignment rather than waiting for help.

      (2) When circulating, most of your interactions with students should be fairly brief.

      (3) Make certain the physical layout of your room facilitates movement among student's desks.

      (4) Have a few extra chairs available so that you can easily sit down if you need to help a student for a short time.

      (5) If students are waiting to be helped, ask them to go on to the next problem if they are able, so that they do not waste time.

Increasing Academic Learning Time

a. Enhance Students' Involvement.

      (1) Attempt to make a correlation between the instructional task and the students' personal lives. Example: "Let's say you wanted to buy a pack of gum at the store; you have 25 cents, but the gum costs 35 cents. How much more do you need?"

(2) Ask students to describe situations where they have needed to use math to solve a problem in their personal lives. For example, ask them to describe a shopping experience.

b. Make Certain Students Attend to Initial Presentations.

(1) Make certain you have eye contact with students when describing lesson content, giving directions, asking questions, and assigning activities.

(2) Make certain that students listen to comments made by other students during small-group discussions.

(3) To make certain that students have attended to information you or another student have presented, ask them to repeat the information back to you in their own words.

c. Involve Students in the Instructional Activity.

(1) Watch for student behaviors that indicate they are involved in the lesson or activity. Such behaviors include listening, responding, reading, writing, and participating in group work.

(2) Ask students questions that confirm whether or not they have been involved in the lesson or instructional activity. "Who, Why, When, Where, and How" questions are usually fairly easy to generate quickly.

d. Provide Relevant Lessons and Assignments.

(1) Avoid giving students "busy work."

(2) Find out what students are interested in and build instructional activities around those interests.

(3) Develop a questionnaire that determines what students are interested in. (This could be part of a writing assignment.)

(4) Focus on teaching students the skills they most need to know in their daily lives, such as time, money, and measurement.

e. Organize Presentations.

(1) Task-analyze the concept or task being presented, paying special attention to the structure and sequencing involved.

(2) Script or outline the steps of the lesson. When you present the lesson, tape-record or videotape it so that you can check to see how well your presentation followed the outline.

(3) Prepare to teach new material in small steps so that the possibility for errors in learning is lessened.

(4) Plan to practice until overlearning occurs. That is, students should continue to practice beyond the point where they can do the task accurately. Automaticity is also important.

(5) Think about whether the concepts, vocabulary, sentence structure, and examples in your presentations are consistent with students' levels of understanding and rate of learning.

(6) Group study, tutorial help, textbooks, workbooks, programmed instruction units, audiovisual methods, and academic games can be used to help organize effective presentations.

(7) Avoid including extraneous material in instructional presentations.

(8) Structure facilitates memory. If new information is presented in a structured manner, students can more easily reconstruct the steps in a given learning process.

(9) Use specific, concrete procedures.

Pacing Curriculum and Lessons

a. Cover an Appropriate Amount of Material.

(1) There is a direct relationship between the amount of material covered and the amount students learn. Establish a yearly schedule for covering the required curriculum.

b. Pace Presentations.

(1) When students repond correctly, comment quickly on their responses and move on.

(2) In most situations, pause no more than one second between questions.

(3) If you are working at an appropriate level of difficulty for a group of students, your expectations of their potential should not greatly affect the pace. That is, even if you are working with a group of students who function below grade level, this doesn't mean that you have to present information at a slower pace, provided you are working at a level they can understand.

(4) Reduce the level of difficulty rather than slow down the pace.

Decreasing Transition Time

a. Prepare Students in Advance.

(1) Warn students about upcoming transitions. A few minutes before a change in activity, warn students that the change is impending. This is especially helpful at the beginning of the school year or the beginning of a new schedule.

(2) Provide students with verbal directions to facilitate transitions. Describe in a step-by-step manner exactly what the expected procedure will be. Transition can involve a physical movement or a change in focus.

(3) Make certain students are attending before giving directions for transitions.

b. Bring Activities to Closure.

   (1) Bring activities to closure before the transition occurs. This can be accomplished by summarizing the main points of the lesson or bringing a halt to a recess activity.

   (2) When students are involved in self-paced activities such as independent practice, let students know every ten minutes or so how much time they have left to work.

c. Establish Routines to Facilitate Transitions.

   (1) Establish a standard set of actions to facilitate transitions. Students need to know clearly what is expected of them. They should be able to make transitions without explicit direction from the teacher.

   (2) Establish a procedure for students who complete work early. This will reduce the amount of time they spend waiting for their classmates to finish assignments.

   (3) When some students finish an assignment early, reinforce those who find something appropriate to do while they are waiting.

d. Manage Student Movement during Transitions.

   (1) Plan for movement transitions within the classroom, out of the classroom, and into the classroom. Consider the number of students involved in the transition: only one student, a group of students, or the entire class.

   (2) For each transition, decide whether students should move from one activity to another individually or as a group.

   (3) Determine whether students need to "line up" to move from one activity to another, or whether they should move independently. Consider the amount of disruptive, inappropriate behavior that occurs with each procedure.

   (4) When students are waiting in line, engage them in a teacher-directed activity. This is a great opportunity for a quick review of math facts or for reciting prose.

   (5) Teach students to bring necessary materials when moving to small-group sessions.

e. Train Students to Respond to Signals.

   (1) Teach students to respond immediately to a signal to move about the room.

   (2) Develop and use the same signal for each transition.

   (3) Establish transition procedures and practice them.

   (4) During the day, keep track of the number and length of transitions. Using a stopwatch can be helpful in keeping track of transition time.

f. Avoid Interruptions.

   (1) Don't allow transition periods to interrupt the flow of the lesson.

   (2) After starting a new activity, don't return to an old one.

(3) Avoid irrelevant announcements and ill-timed inter-jections.

(4) Be prepared to manage two types of transitions: student transitions (sharpening a pencil, getting a drink of water) and teacher transitions (locating a set of worksheets, answering a telephone call).

(5) When working with a group of students, don't spend excessive time with any one student.

(6) Don't digress or get sidetracked on irrelevant issues.

(7) Following student responses, continue quickly with the presentation.

(8) Save time by collecting papers after students have started the next activity.

F. Self-improvement Plan: Time Management

After completing the self-evaluation checklist (Section C) and reading through the practical suggestions (Section E), you should be prepared to develop a self-improvement plan (SIP). Please complete portion A, entitled "Time Management: Goals and Objectives," on the self-improvement plan, by checking the goal(s) and objectives(s) you wish to include in your plan. Also, write a brief narrative describing your plan, to address the requirements in portions B–E. (An example of a filled-in SIP is provided following the blank one.)

Self-improvement Plan: Time Management

Name _____ Class _____ Date _____

A. Time Management: Goals and Objectives
Which of the following goals and objectives will you focus on?

1. Increase Allocated Time
  a. Keep sufficient materials and supplies available.
  b. Have necessary equipment and supplies available.
  c. Keep materials and equipment easily accessible.
  d. Plan the collection and correction of homework.
  e. Other _____

2. Increase Engaged Time
  a. Begin classwork on schedule.
  b. Get the attention of the class.
  c. Get the class started after breaks in the schedule.
  d. Use nondisruptive signals to get students involved.
  e. Focus students' attention on instructional tasks.
  f. Circulate around the room.
  g. Other _____

3. Increase Academic Learning Time
  a. Enhance students' involvement.
  b. Make certain students attend to initial presentations.
  c. Involve students in the instructional activity.
  d. Provide relevant lessons and assignments.
  e. Organize presentations.
  f. Other _____

4. Pace Curriculum and Lessons
  a. Cover an appropriate amount of material.
  b. Pace presentations.
  c. Other _____

5. Decrease Transition Time
  a. Prepare students in advance.
  b. Bring activities to closure.
  c. Establish routines to facilitate transitions.
  d. Manage student movement during transitions.
  e. Train students to respond to signals.
  f. Avoid interruptions.
  g. Other _____

B. Practical Suggestions

Please indicate which of the practical suggestions from Section E you plan to use to meet each of the objectives. (You may include practical suggestions from other sources as well.)

C. Specific Procedures

Please describe the specific procedures you will use to implement the practical suggestions.

D. Current and Desired Performance

Please describe your current performance and desired performance in regard to each of the objectives you have selected. You may state the performance in terms of student behavior, such as percentage of engaged time.

E. Timelines and Change Measures

Please describe your timelines and how you will measure change in relationship to the objective(s) you have selected.

F. Results

Upon completion of your self-improvement project, write a brief description of the results of the implementation. Attach any raw data sheets that were used to gather information and describe any changes that were made during your project.

Sample Self-improvement Plan: Time Management

Name _Mike R._ Class _Math_ Date _2/6/89_

A. Time Management: Goals and Objectives
Which of the following goals and objectives will you focus on?

1. Increase Allocated Time
   a. Keep sufficient materials and supplies available.
   b. Have necessary equipment and supplies available.
   c. Keep materials and equipment easily accessible.
   d. Plan the collection and correction of homework.
   e. Other _____

✓ 2. Increase Engaged Time
   a. Begin classwork on schedule.
   b. Get the attention of the class.
   c. Get the class started after breaks in the schedule.
   d. Use nondisruptive signals to get students involved.
   e. Focus students' attention on instructional tasks.
   ✓ **f.** Circulate around the room.
   g. Other _____

3. Increase Academic Learning Time
   a. Enhance students' involvement.
   b. Make certain students attend to initial presentations.
   c. Involve students in the instructional activity.
   d. Provide relevant lessons and assignments.
   e. Organize presentations.
   f. Other _____

4. Pace Curriculum and Lessons
   a. Cover an appropriate amount of material.
   b. Pace presentations.
   c. Other _____

✓ 5. Decrease Transition Time
   a. Prepare students in advance.
   b. Bring activities to closure.
   c. Establish routines to facilitate transitions.
   d. Manage student movement during transitions.
   ✓ **e.** Train students to respond to signals.
   f. Avoid interruptions.
   g. Other _____

B. Practical Suggestions

To meet my objective of circulating around the room, I will implement the following practical suggestions:

   1. I will make certain the physical layout of my room facilitates movement among students' desks.

   2. I will make certain that most of my interactions with students are fairly brief.

C. Specific Procedures

   1. I will draw a floor plan, as it is now, and a plan of how a more accessible layout would look. I will rearrange the furniture according to the new plan.

   2. I will monitor the length of time I spend with each student while circulating. I will spend 15 seconds or less with each student.

D. Current and Desired Performance

   1. *Currently,* the layout of my classroom does not facilitate movement among students' desks. I *desire* to be able to move quickly from one side of the room to the other within three seconds.

   2. *Currently,* I am spending too much time (5–10 minutes) with a few students who are having more difficulty than the others. Consequently, the other students get off-task. I *desire* to be able to spend less time with each student per contact, but to make more contacts (20–25) than I am now making (5–6 per independent practice session).

E. Timelines and Change Measures

   1. I will change the layout of my classroom in one week from the date of this report. I will submit the floor plans as evidence of the change.

   2. I will consistently make brief contacts with students by the end of the next three weeks. I will monitor the number of times I spend more than 15 seconds with a student during independent practice sessions. I will keep a frequency count on an index card I carry in my pocket.

F. Results

   1. The change in room arrangement was most helpful (see attached floor plans).

   2. It was difficult to limit contacts initially, but I found that by giving the slower students more guided practice, independent practice went a lot more smoothly (see attached data sheets).

References

Berliner, D.C. (1984). The half-full glass: A review of research on teaching. In P.L. Hosford (Ed.), *Using what we know about teaching* (pp. 51–77), Alexandria, Va: Association for Supervision and Curriculum Development.

Borg, W.R. (1980). Time and school learning. In C. Denham & A. Lieberman (Eds.), *Time to learn* (pp. 33–72). Washington, D.C.: U.S. Department of Education, National Institute of Education.

Brophy, J. (1986, April). *Teacher effects research and teacher quality.* Paper presented at the annual meeting of the American Educational Research Association, San Francisco.

Buchmann, M., & Schmidt, W.H. (1981). *The school day and the teachers' content commitments* (IRT Research Series #83). East Lansing, Mich.: Michigan State University, Institute for Research on Teaching.

Doyle, P.H. (1986). Classroom organization and management. In M.C. Wittrock (Ed.), *Handbook of research on teaching,* 3rd ed. (pp. 392–431). New York: Macmillan.

Fisher, C.W., Berliner, D.C., Filby, N.N., Marliave, R., Cahen, L.S., & Dishaw, M.M. (1980). Teaching behaviors, academic learning time, and student achievement: An overview. In C. Denham & A. Lieberman (Eds.), *Time to learn* (pp. 7–32). Washington, D.C.: U.S. Department of Education, National Institute of Education.

Good, T.L., Grouws, D.A., & Ebmeier, H. (1983). *Active mathematics teaching.* New York: Longman.

Gump, P.S. (1967). *The classroom behavior setting: Its nature and relationship to student behavior (final report).* Washington, D.C.: U.S. Office of Education, Bureau of Research. (ERIC Document Reproduction Service No. ED 015 515.)

Kounin, J.S., & Doyle, P.H. (1975). Degree of continuity of a lesson's signal system and the task involvement of children. *Journal of Educational Psychology, 67,* 159–164.

Latham G. (1985). *A data-based approach to assessing program quality.* Unpublished manuscript, Utah State University, Mountain Plains Regional Resource Center, Logan. Utah.

Marliave, R., & Filby, N.N. (1985). Success rate: A measure of task appropriateness. In C.W. Fisher & D.C. Berliner (Eds.), *Perspectives on instructional time* (pp. 217–235). New York: Longman.

Romberg, T.A. (1980). Salient features of the BTES framework of teacher behaviors. In C. Denham & A. Lieberman (Eds.), *Time to learn* (pp. 73–93). Washington, D.C.: Department of Health, Education, and Welfare, National Institute of Education.

Rosenshine, B. (1980). How time is spent in elementary classrooms. In C. Denham & A. Lieberman (Eds.), *Time to learn* (pp. 107–126). Washington, D.C.: U.S. Department of Education, National Institute of Education.

Ross, R.P. (1983). *What's happening in elementary school classrooms? Research on time use, classroom operations, and activity management* (Report No. PS 014567). Urbana, Ill.: University of Illinois, College of Education, ERIC Clearing House on Elementary and Early Childhood Education.

Stallings, J.A. (1975, March/April). *Relationships between classroom instructional practices on child development.* Paper presented at the annual meeting of the American Educational Research Association, Washington, D.C. (ERIC Document Reproduction Service No. ED 110 200.)

Wiley, D.E., & Harnischfeger, A. (1974). Explosion of a myth: Quantity of schooling and exposure to instruction, major educational vehicles. *Educational Researcher, 3*(4), 7–12.

Wyne, M.D., Stuck, G.B., White, K.P., & Coop, R.H. (1986). *Carolina teaching performance assessment system.* Chapel Hill, N.C.: University of North Carolina, Group for the Study of Effective Teaching, School of Education.

CHAPTER 3

Teaching Functions

A. The Research Literature
   Teaching Function Concepts
   Getting It All Together to Meet Student Needs
B. Knowledge Quiz: Teaching Functions
   Answer Key: Knowledge Quiz (Teaching Functions)
C. Self-evaluation Checklist: Teaching Functions
   Instructions for Completing the Self-evaluation
      Checklist
   Self-evaluation Checklist
D. Information Gathering: Teaching Functions
   Analyzing Instructional Presentations
   The Review Game
   Speaking Clearly and Fluently
E. Practical Suggestions: Teaching Functions
   Daily, Weekly, and Monthly Reviews
   Presentation of New Content
   Guided Student Practice
F. Self-improvement Plan: Teaching Functions
References

A. The Research Literature

In this chapter, the term *teaching functions* refers to classroom experiences that serve to move students from a lack of mastery to mastery in an academic content area. Descriptions of the most effective teaching functions usually leave little doubt about the specific student learning experiences fostered by the teacher's behavior. Doyle (1985) noted that it is the instructional function served (e.g., to increase guided practice), not the teaching behavior, that is most important.

Rosenshine and Stevens' (1986) synthesis of the research provides the following summary statement on teaching functions:

> In general, researchers have found that when effective teachers teach well structured subjects, they
>
> 1. begin a lesson with a short review of previous, prerequisite learning.
> 2. begin a lesson with a short statement of goals.
> 3. present new material in small steps, with student practice after each step.
> 4. give clear and detailed instructions and explanations.
> 5. provide a high level of active practice for all students.
> 6. ask a large number of questions, check for student understanding, and obtain responses from all students.
> 7. guide students during initial practice.
> 8. provide systematic feedback and corrections.
> 9. provide explicit instruction and practice for seatwork exercises and, where necessary, monitor students during seatwork.
>
> The major components in systematic teaching include teaching in small steps (with student practice after each step), guiding students during initial practice, and providing all students with a high level of successful practice. Of course, all teachers use some of these behaviors some of the time, but the most effective teachers use most of them almost all the time [p. 377].

Good and Grouws (1979) found that when teachers increased their emphasis on the following five teaching functions, their students achieved more than students of teachers who did not emphasize them.

1. Check the previous day's work and reteach where necessary.
2. Present new content or skills, proceeding rapidly but in small steps, while giving detailed instructions and explanations.

3. Have students practice the material while providing feedback and corrections.
4. Have students do independent practice.
5. Provide weekly and monthly reviews.

The presence of the teaching functions is important, but the timing and amount of time devoted to each function is also significant. For example, guided practice is important, but only if it is conducted at the right time and for long enough to ensure that the student error rate is low before engaging in independent practice. The timing and amount of each activity must be related to its effect on students.

In commenting on the teaching functions highlighted by the research on effective teachers, Rosenshine and Stevens (1986) noted that the specific functions are consistent with the theoretical recommendations of Gagne (1970), the practical guidance from Hunter's essential elements for lesson design (Hunter & Russell, 1981), and a wide range of research findings on the procedures used by effective teachers.

Teaching Function Concepts

The majority of teaching functions considered important by researchers have been consolidated into the following five groups: (a) daily reviews and prerequisite checks, (b) presentation of new content, (c) guided student practice, (d) independent student practice, and (e) weekly and monthly reviews (see Figure 3.1).

1. Daily Reviews and Prerequisite Checks. Typically, the effective teacher will initiate a lesson with a series of related activities that will serve to (a) review the material covered in the previous lesson, (b) check on homework, and (c) check on the prerequisite skills needed for the new content that will be covered in the lesson.

Daily reviews. One of the most effective ways to initiate a lesson is to review the previous lesson by presenting two or three problems that require a written response by all students. If these problems are on the screen, chalkboard, or worksheet in front of the students when they enter the classroom, and if all the students are actively responding to the problems within the first sixty seconds of the lesson, a number of important things happen, including:

a. A work-oriented tone is established. If a lesson starts with a long, rambling discourse by the teacher and passive participation by students, a very different tone may be set for the lesson.
b. Since the review problems cover material previously taught, the error rate should be low. This means that most students will start the lesson on a successful note. Consistent demonstra-

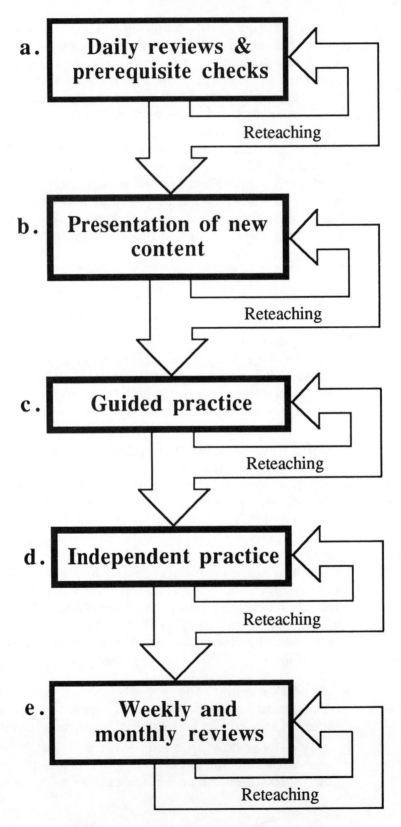

FIGURE 3.1

Major Teaching Functions

a. Daily reviews & prerequisite checks

Reteaching

b. Presentation of new content

Reteaching

c. Guided practice

Reteaching

d. Independent practice

Reteaching

e. Weekly and monthly reviews

Reteaching

tions of success are one of the best ways to facilitate the development of appropriate attitudes toward the content and the instruction.

c. Since there are often class management problems associated with transitions between lessons, and since some of these may have to do with factors outside the teacher's classroom, the teacher is in a good position to deal with problems if the majority of students are actively engaged in responding to the review problems at the start of a lesson.

d. Most class management issues are usually associated with a few students who come to class without any interest in participating. If these students get the message within the first minute of class that they will be expected to participate and that the teacher will take the time to check on them individually, then management problems will be reduced.

Homework. There is a lack of consensus in the research literature on the importance of large amounts of homework, but there is some agreement on the importance of the following guidelines:

a. Requiring a session of at least fifteen minutes per night per subject is helpful.

b. The homework should serve to consolidate and review.

c. Students should not be encountering new material or have high error rates in homework assignments.

d. Homework should be checked promptly.

Prerequisite skills. One of the characteristics of a master teacher is the appropriate treatment of prerequisite skills. The master teacher knows what new material is likely to be difficult for students and which prerequisite skills are important for the successful introduction of new material. Rather than place students in remedial situations, the master teacher will try to prevent errors and misconcepts by making sure that the new material is introduced in small steps and that students demonstrate mastery of the critical prerequisite skills before starting the sequence of small steps.

Prerequisite skills are typically considered at the start of a course of study and at the beginning of each lesson that introduces new content. Most effective teachers use a combination of group and individual instruction. Group instruction can be very effective if the teacher assesses the students at the beginning of the course to determine how the skills they bring to the class will match up with the course curriculum. The appropriate management of prerequisite skills calls for an in-depth understanding of instruction, curriculum, and student learning. Such understanding does not come easily; it is characteristic of an individual who has made a major commitment to the science and art of teaching.

The prerequisites needed to ensure high levels of success in the early stages of acquiring new knowledge include (a) skills mastered to automaticity, (b) problem-solving strategies, and (c) general principles and concepts (see Figure 3.2).

FIGURE 3.2

Making Instruction Meaningful: The Role of Reviews and Prerequisites

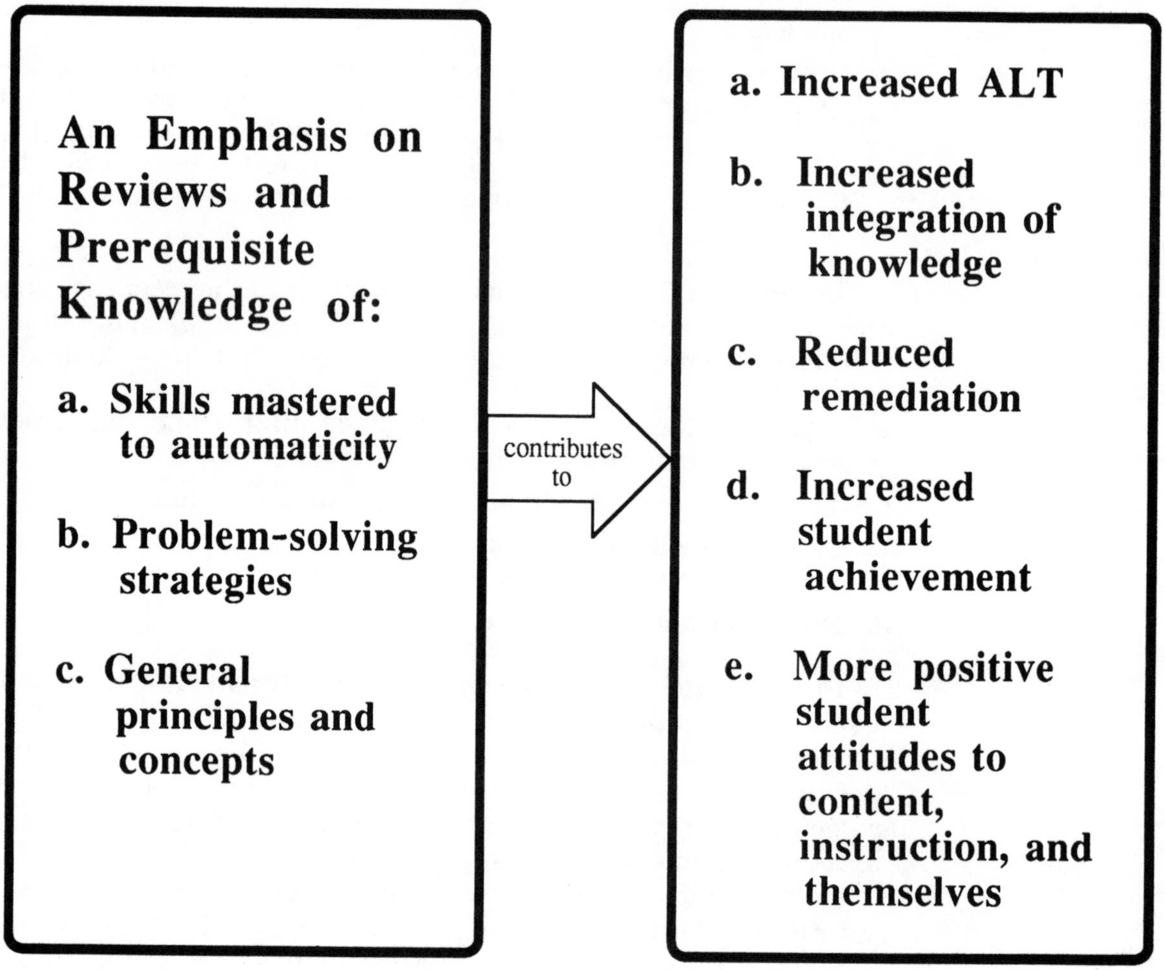

| An Emphasis on Reviews and Prerequisite Knowledge of:

a. Skills mastered to automaticity

b. Problem-solving strategies

c. General principles and concepts | contributes to → | a. Increased ALT

b. Increased integration of knowledge

c. Reduced remediation

d. Increased student achievement

e. More positive student attitudes to content, instruction, and themselves |

a. **Skills mastered to automaticity.** One should not be teaching complex algorithmic procedures, such as long division, if students are struggling with the prerequisite facts in subtraction and multiplication. Lessons in reading comprehension will have little value if the needed decoding skills have not been mastered.

b. **Problem-solving strategies.** Even the simplest of work problems requires the mastery of strategies to determine what information is provided and what information is needed to solve the problems. Such strategies will be prerequisites for more advanced word problems.

c. **General principles and concepts.** Commenting on earlier research on the difference between novice and expert problem solving in physics, Doyle (1985, p.64) stated, "a teacher needs to describe the connections between lessons, in order to build broad understandings of content and place individual tasks within a wider context of understanding. In addition, a teacher needs to design tasks that require students to integrate information across individual lessons and class sessions." In the teaching of earth science, the convection cell is a concept that helps explain the movement of air in the atmosphere, the deep ocean currents, and the movement of magma inside the earth. Once taught, the concept of the convection cell will be prerequisite knowledge to help integrate information across several earth science topics. Doyle noted that the better problem solvers possessed "domain-specific knowledge in the subject area" and could interpret problems in terms of the underlying principles and concepts.

Reteaching. Student errors should be minimal for daily reviews, homework checks, and prerequisite skill checks. All these activities involve previously taught material. If most of the students do not demonstrate mastery, reteaching should be conducted immediately. Certainly one would not want to introduce any new material if less than 80 percent of the class did not demonstrate mastery of important prerequisite skills. It would be far better to spend the rest of the class period teaching the prerequisite skills. Rather than place a large percentage of the class in a remedial situation, it would be better to delay the new material a day so as to help ensure initial success once it is introduced.

Because remedial instruction is expensive in teacher and student time, and destructive for the attitudes of both students and teacher, there is no economy of time or effort in the premature introduction of new material.

2. Presentation of New Content. Evertson, Emmer, and Brophy (1980), writing in the *Journal of Research in Mathematics Education*, reported that the most effective teachers spend about twenty-three minutes per day on the presentation of new material through demonstrations, discussions, and lectures. The least effective teachers spend only eleven minutes per day on the same activities.

The following guidelines for presenting new material were prepared by Rosenshine and Stevens (1986, p. 381), based upon their review of the research literature.

1. Clarity of goals and main points.
   a. State the goals or objectives of the presentation.
   b. Focus on one thought (point, direction) at a time.
   c. Avoid digressions.
   d. Avoid ambiguous phrases and pronouns.
2. Step-by-step presentations.
   a. Present the material in small steps.

    b. Organize and present the material so that one point is mastered before the next point is given.

    c. Give explicit, step-by-step directions (when possible).

    d. Present an outline when the material is complex.

3. Specific and concrete procedures.

    a. Model the skill or process (when appropriate).

    b. Give detailed and redundant explanations for difficult points.

    c. Provide students with concrete and varied examples.

4. Checking for students' understanding.

    a. Be sure that students understand one point before proceeding to the next point.

    b. Ask the students questions to monitor their comprehension of what has been presented.

    c. Have students summarize the main points in their own words.

    d. Reteach the parts of the presentation that the students have difficulty comprehending, either by further teaching explanation or by students tutoring other students.

Clarity of presentation is emerging as an important component of all aspects of the presentation of new content. Brophy (1987) wrote,

> Students achieve more when their teachers make clear presentations marked by continuity and precision of language rather than interruptions due to false starts or meandering into side issues, hemming and hawing, or vague terminology. Most of the presently available information is on factors that detract from clarity, although recent work has begun to develop methods of conceptualizing and measuring positive aspects of clarity such as sufficiency of definitions, accuracy of examples, and explicitness of explanations [p. IV-133].

3. Guided Student Practice. Guided student practice serves as a bridge between activities designed to present new material and independent student practice. The guided student practice is integrated into activities designed to present new material. In math instruction, for example, guided practice could involve having the student practice one or several steps in the algorithm used to solve a single calculation or problem. In the more advanced stages of presenting new material, guided practice could involve the presentation of several math problems and the associated feedback procedures.

    Guided practice and independent practice represent different points on a single continuum, so no absolute dividing point can be established to discriminate between the two related activities. Guided practice should be conducted in small steps and should be intensely supervised. It should prevent the development of consistent error patterns and inappropriate practices. This means that guided practice must be designed and implemented so that errors are identified and reteaching conducted immediately.

Hunter (1984), in discussing the importance of guided practice, stressed the need for students to practice their new knowledge or skill *under direct teacher supervision*. Hunter further noted that "New learning is like wet cement; it is easily damaged. An error at the beginning of learning can be easily 'set' so that it is harder to eradicate than had it been apprehended immediately" (p. 176).

The research literature has consistently stressed the importance of appropriate amounts of guided practice for all learners, but nowhere is this guided practice more important than with low achievers. It has been noted that "The important element seems to be the provision of controlled practice with positive teacher feedback" (Voelker Morsink, Chase Thomas, & Smith-Davis, 1987, p. 292). The fact that certain members of the class will require more guided practice than others suggests that each lesson should contain a certain amount of time in which the higher-achieving students are working on independent practice, while the teacher is working closely with low-achieving students on guided practice.

The effectiveness of guided practice can be evaluated by measures of student success in independent practice. If students are at least 80 percent successful when they begin the subsequent independent practice, then guided practice has been appropriately conducted.

4. Independent Practice. In learning a new skill or concept, the students progress through two phases: acquisition and consolidation. Teaching activities designed to support the presentation of new content and guided student practice contribute to the acquisition phase; activities concerned with review and independent student practice contribute to the consolidation phase.

The transition from guided practice to independent practice should not occur until students are at least 80 percent successful in their guided practice. The independent practice should continue past the point at which the student is 100 percent successful. Independent practice should continue until the use of the skills becomes automatic.

Samuels (1981) identified two levels of independent practice: a *unitization* level and an *automaticity* level. At the unitization level, the students are integrating their skills with previous knowledge. They make few errors, but learning is not easy; they usually get the right answer with a considerable investment of effort. At the automaticity level, the students are performing the skills successfully, easily, and without having to think through the steps involved in performing the skill. When the automaticity level has been reached, the skill has been *overlearned*. Rosenshine and Stevens (1986) made the following observation with regard to the importance of overlearning:

Overlearning is particularly important for hierarchical materials such as mathematics and elementary reading. Unless there is overlearning to the point of automaticity, it is unlikely that the material will be retained. Furthermore, hierarchical material requires the application of previously learned skills to subsequent new skills. The advantage of automaticity is that students who master the material can then concentrate their attention on learning new skills or applying the skills to new situations. For example, automaticity of decoding skills frees the students' attention for comprehension, just as automaticity of computation frees the students' attention for mathematical problem solving [p. 386].

5. Weekly and Monthly Reviews. There are two types of reviews: (1) daily reviews and (2) weekly and monthly reviews. As previously discussed, daily reviews facilitate the introduction of new content. The weekly and monthly reviews are designed to ensure that content previously mastered is not forgotten. Good and Grouws (1979) noted that effective teachers were devoting between 15 and 20 percent of instructional time to weekly and monthly reviews.

A weekly comprehensive mastery test can serve the dual purpose of reviewing material and providing a valid measure of student progress for grading purposes. A test that diagnoses how much material a student is retaining is also providing the teacher with feedback on the quality of instruction. If certain skills are consistently giving large numbers of students problems on mastery tests of retention, the teacher must reexamine the instructional presentation and student practice activities that were associated with the acquisition and consolidation of the skill.

Getting It All Together to Meet Student Needs

Adjusting Resources. The point has been made by Rosenshine and Stevens (1986) that all teachers will at some time use all the important teaching function skills. The effective teacher is the individual who uses the skills in the right amount at the right time, in response to student needs.

Individualized instruction is not primarily concerned with the physical individualization of the instructional setting; rather, it stresses the monitoring of students as individuals to ensure that instruction, whether in group or individual settings, is consistent with their needs.

Noli (1980) noted:

Student engagement rates are higher when students are involved in more academic interaction with the instructor. Engagement rates are higher in a group setting than during independent seatwork. Engagement rates are higher when students receive more monitoring or help from an instructor [p. 220].

The teacher has to balance the facility of group settings to ensure high engagement with the facility of individual settings to match instruction to different student needs. The more diverse the entering skills of students, the more difficult the balancing process will be.

In an overview of the research on practices that foster student learning, it was noted that

> It will not be suitable to use one organizational pattern for the entire day . . . . The teacher must devise some workable system using different settings (group work and seat work) for different students in different content areas at different times during the day, and keep the whole system adaptable to changes in student needs during the year [Fisher et al., 1980, p. 32].

Table 3.1 is an example of how a fifty-minute period might be used to ensure an appropriate balance among teaching functions, group instruction, and seatwork to meet the needs of all students in a timely fashion.

During Segments 1 and 2, the teacher would spend time on the classroom floor monitoring student performance to determine which students need additional guided practice during Segment 3. If major problems were detected in Segment 1, the teacher would delay the introduction of new content and reteach the prerequisite skills.

The lesson structure in Table 3.1 assumes that the teacher assessed the entry skills at the beginning of the course to ensure that all students could benefit from the course of instruction.

The scheduling of independent practice as the final segment of a lesson helps minimize the management problems associated with the physical individualization of instructional settings. These management problems were documented by Copeland (1987) as follows:

> The degree of multiplicity of dimensions, immediacy, and simultaneity required to keep 25 students highly involved in the

TABLE 3.1   Example of a Lesson Schedule

Lesson Segment	Time	Instructional Setting	Teaching Function
1	5-10 minutes	Group	Review and check on prerequisites.
2	20-25 minutes	Group	Presentation of new content integrated with guided practice.
3	20-25 minutes	Individual	Independent practice for average and above-average students. Additional guided practice for low achievers.

number of different activities necessary for individualization may put such tasks beyond the information-processing capacity of many teachers. If so, teachers' often-observed inability to implement highly structured recommendations for individualization may be better understood [pp. 234–235].

By scheduling the independent seatwork and additional guided practice after the group presentation of new content and associated guided practice, the following is achieved:

a. The majority of the class is working relatively independently on the same set of skills.

b. The error rate for most students will be low, because most are doing independent, not guided practice.

c. If students experience a smooth transition with well-prepared materials, the entry into independent practice should not have been disruptive.

d. By this time in the lesson, the teacher should have a good understanding of which students have problems.

The end result should be a classroom that is easier to supervise than a classroom in which the individual instruction occurred earlier, or one in which the introduction of new content was being conducted in individual settings.

Safety Nets and Individual Differences. Individual differences certainly give rise to management problems. There seems to be a widespread misconception that all individual differences come from the individual student. In fact, the breadth of individual differences is a function of both the contributions of the individual and the quality of instruction. An educational system should not be repressing the unique essence of the individual, nor should it be creating individual differences in achievement by failing to address individual knowledge deficits in a timely manner.

Block (1980) called for more emphasis on a "self-correcting system of schooling." He noted that many existing practices are "error-promoting" and require that

> Educators must give special attention to a wider range of learner management problems. They must, for example, "individualize" their instruction in the face of unnecessarily wide ranges of individual differences in students' readiness to learn. This typically entails redoing portions of their predecessors' jobs as well as trying to do their own [p. 98].

The message is clear. All teachers must make certain they have a systematic set of classroom practices that ensure that errors are detected and reteaching conducted in a timely manner. Such detection and reteaching will

a. Reduce future classroom management problems by reducing unnecessary individual differences

b. Promote student achievement and more positive student attitudes by providing more consistent demonstrations of success

c. Provide a more effective working environment for colleagues receiving the students

Daily Safety Nets. A safety net has two components: error detection and reteaching. A daily safety net can be established by ensuring that every lesson is systematically planned so that errors can be detected and reteaching conducted based on these errors. For example, in the lesson structure shown in Table 3.1, there is an opportunity for error detection and reteaching in Segment 1. Even more important will be the error detection and reteaching that occurs in Segments 2 and 3. If more than 20 percent of the class experience difficulty with the introduction of new content, reteaching should be conducted immediately. If only a few students are experiencing problems, the teacher may note the students; during Segment 3, the teacher will be free to provide additional guided practice with these few children while the others work independently on prepared seatwork activities. With such a safety net, even the students who have major problems will receive reteaching that addresses their needs within the same lesson that the problems were detected.

The maintenance of daily safety nets does not come easily. It requires a mobile, alert teacher, constantly monitoring the high-risk students. Also necessary are well-prepared practice materials that will provide meaningful experiences for the majority while the teacher spends time with students in difficulty during the last part of each lesson. The quality of the salvage program will be consistent with the physical and cognitive energy expended by the teacher.

Weekly and Monthly Safety Nets. As noted earlier, the more effective teachers systematically set aside 15 to 20 percent of the allocated time for weekly and monthly reviews. In the study conducted by Good, Grouws, and Ebmeier (1983), one day each week (usually Monday) was set aside for weekly and monthly reviews. For three of these review days each month, the teachers emphasized the content covered in the previous week. On one day each month, the teachers emphasized the content covered during the previous month. If each of these review days is initiated by a diagnostic test of the content covered during the previous week or month, the test itself will serve as a review, and the teacher will have the information needed to conduct reteaching for the remainder of the lesson. If major problems are encountered, the teacher may continue the reteaching into the next lesson. By keeping track of the problems encountered during the weekly reviews, the teacher will be able to develop well-targeted diagnostic tests for the monthly reviews.

Planning for Differences. Some students require more practice than others (Block, 1980). One strategy for varying the amount of practice is to prepare three parallel sets of practice examples for each lesson. Although each set of examples is different, each covers the same concepts at the same level of difficulty. One set is used during the guided practice that all students participate in (see Segment 2 in Table 3.1). The second set is used during the last part of the lesson (see Segment 3 in Table 3.1), while most of the students are experiencing independent practice and several students are receiving guided practice. For homework, the students who were doing independent practice in Segment 2 complete the second set for homework. The students who used the second set for guided practice then complete the third set for homework.

The practice of preparing three parallel sets of examples will accomplish two important objectives. First, it facilitates a successful transition from guided to independent practice. The probability of success in independent practice will increase, because the same problem types will have been encountered and practiced during the preceding guided practice. Second, those students in need of extra practice will receive it, with examples that emphasize conceptual understanding rather than rote learning. Repeated practice with the same set of examples would emphasize rote learning.

Expectation of Success. The research literature has noted that effective instructional programs are characterized by an *expectation of success*, which can be facilitated if

a. The teacher confidently and briskly presents a carefully validated sequence of instruction.

b. The students experience recurring demonstrations of success, particularly in the initial stages of learning a skill.

Effective teachers have been described as "those who almost never use criticism; they have and communicate high expectation; present task-oriented instruction, reinforce on-task behavior, and use high rates of the contingent praise" (Voelker Morsink, Chase Thomas, & Smith-Davis, 1987, p. 291).

In essence, the critical attributes of a classroom climate that has an expectation of success include:

a. Proven successful curriculum sequences and teaching methods

b. Consistent success experiences

c. Consistent and timely recognition of student success

Compromises and Reality. Brophy (1987) summarized one of the realities of teaching as follows:

> The total instructional program will be a compromise constructed in the belief that it will allow the teacher to meet more of the needs of more of the students than any of the feasible alternatives—it will not be an ideal program that continually meets each individual student's needs. The need to accept compromises by trading off classroom management benefits against costs in instructional quality and efficiency increases in relationship to the size and heterogeneity of the class [p. IV-123].

Lightfoot (1983), in her analysis of the characteristics of effective secondary schools, noted that a concern for the weakest members of the school community was a characteristic common to the effective schools she observed. It is important that safety nets and similar strategies be integrated and accepted instructional components as teachers confront the compromises and realities of teaching. Such demonstrated concern for the weaker members of the school community creates a beneficial affective and academic climate for all.

B. Knowledge Quiz: Teaching Functions

Multiple Choice

Question 1

a. Guided practice is conducted until learning is automatic.
b. Guided practice is a part of independent learning activities.
c. Guided practice is integrated with other content presentation activities.
d. Guided practice is included with most daily reviews.

Question 2   Research indicates that effective teachers present new material through lectures, discussions, and demonstrations for

a. 10 to 15 minutes per day.
b. 15 to 20 minutes per day.
c. 20 to 25 minutes per day.
d. 25 to 30 minutes per day.

Question 3   The concept of overlearning is associated with

a. guided practice.
b. independent practice.
c. daily reviews.
d. monthly reviews.

Question 4   Instruction in prerequisite skills is best stressed

a. when students fail.
b. as a part of guided practice.
c. as a part of independent practice.
d. at the beginning of the lesson.

Question 5   One way to determine the effectiveness of guided practice is to

a. determine the amount of time given to it.
b. determine the level of success in subsequent independent practice.
c. see if prerequisite skills are mastered.
d. see if it is associated with demonstrations.

Question 6 Student engagement is easier in

a. individual settings.
b. group settings.
c. during transitions.
d. independent practice.

Question 7 Individualized instruction emphasizes

a. the use of physical individualization.
b. the use of individual work stations.
c. the use of tutorial approaches to match instruction to needs.
d. the monitoring of individuals to match instruction to needs.

Question 8 Effective classrooms are characterized by

a. the expectation of success.
b. a highly affective climate.
c. open architecture.
d. an authoritarian climate.

Question 9 The most appropriate time to identify student errors is during

a. independent practice.
b. homework.
c. guided practice.
d. overlearning.

Question 10 Classroom activities should provide

a. equal guided practice for all.
b. varying amounts of guided practice based on student performance.
c. equal amounts of independent practice.
d. similar amounts of guided and independent practice.

Fill in the Blanks

Question 11   In assessing a classroom practice, the instructional _____ is more important than the teacher behavior.

Question 12   Prerequisites include:

a. _____

b. _____

c. _____

Question 13   The breadth of individual differences in achievement is generated by the individual and the _____.

Question 14   A "safety net" has two components:

a. _____

b. _____

Question 15   Weekly and monthly reviews should be conducted _____ day/s per _____.

Answer Key: Knowledge Quiz (Teaching Functions)

Multiple Choice

Question 1

c. Guided practice is integrated with other content presentation activities.

Question 2 Research indicates that effective teachers present new material through lectures, discussions, and demonstrations

c. 20 to 25 minutes per day.

Question 3 The concept of overlearning is associated with

b. independent practice.

Question 4 Instruction in prerequisite skills is best stressed

d. at the beginning of the lesson.

Question 5 One way to determine the effectiveness of guided practice is to

b. determine the level of success in subsequent independent practice.

Question 6 Student engagement is easier in

b. group settings.

Question 7 Individualized instruction emphasizes

d. the monitoring of individuals to match instruction to needs.

Question 8 Effective classrooms are characterized by

a. the expectation of success.

Question 9 The most appropriate time to identify student errors is during

c. guided practice.

Question 10 Classroom activities should provide

b. varying amounts of guided practice based on student performance.

Question 11
In assessing a classroom practice, the instructional *function* is more important than the teacher behavior.

Question 12 Prerequisites include:

a. *skills mastered to automaticity*
b. *problem-solving strategies*
c. *general principles and concepts*

Question 13
The breadth of individual differences in achievement is generated by the individual and the *quality of instruction.*

Question 14 A "safety net" has two components:

a. *error detection*
b. *reteaching*

Question 15
Weekly and monthly reviews should be conducted *one* day/s per week.

C. Self-evaluation Checklist: Teaching Functions

Instructions for Completing the Self-evaluation Checklist

The self-evaluation checklist on the following pages should be completed using the following scale and criteria.

1 = No change is needed in present practices.

2 = There are minor problems that can be corrected quickly and easily.

3 = There are major problems that will require a considerable investment in time and effort.

4 = I need more specific information on my own behavior before I can decide whether I have a problem.

The evaluation questions are provided as a guide to the type of specific behaviors that exemplify each of the effective teaching skills. You should feel free to add evaluation questions if you feel that they will increase the practicality and sensitivity of the evaluation process. In many cases, extra space has been provided to allow for added evaluation questions.

Please make supporting notes that will help describe any problems in more detail. Notes should address the context; for example, certain problems may be more or less important, depending on the time, the class, the individual student, the lesson activity, and the subject being taught.

If the space provided on the evaluation checklist is not sufficient, supplement the checklist by adding descriptive material and cross-referencing supplementary material with the number of the skill and the letter of the evaluation question (e.g., Skill 2, Question c.).

Additional information on the criteria and the use of the self-evaluation checklist is provided in Section C of Chapter 2.

Self-evaluation Checklist

Skill 1. Daily Reviews
Daily reviews and prerequisite checks are conducted systematically and effectively.

Evaluation Questions	Rating and Notes	
a. Do most lessons include a short review of skills taught in previous lessons?		
b. Does the review include an assessment of the level of mastery of skills reviewed?		
c. Do you often get well into the body of a lesson and find you have to reteach prerequisites?		
d. On reviews, do you immediately reteach if less than 80 percent demonstrate mastery?		

Skill 2. New Content
A major part of most lessons is set aside for the effective acquisition of new content.

Evaluation Questions	Rating and Notes	
a. Is extensive guided practice integrated into demonstrations and lectures on new content?		
b. Is approximately half the lesson time devoted to guided practice, demonstrations, and presentations of new content?		
c. Do you monitor guided practice and conduct reteaching if necessary?		
d. Do you revise instruction if students consistently experience difficulty?		
e. Is the material taught in small steps, with performance checks after each step?		

Rating Scale: 1 - No change; 2 - Minor problems; 3 - Major problems; 4 - Insufficient information

Skill 3. Independent Practice
Independent practice is consistently and effectively conducted.

Evaluation Questions	Rating and Notes	
a. Are the students achieving better than 80 percent before moving from guided to independent practice?		
b. Is a minimum of 20 minutes of independent practice assigned on most days in each major subject area?		
c. Do students receive prompt feedback on independent practice?		
d. Is independent practice extensive enough to achieve "overlearning"?		

Skill 4. Comprehensive Mastery Testing
Mastery testing is conducted systematically and diagnostically.

Evaluation Questions	Rating and Notes	
a. Is comprehensive mastery testing conducted at least twice per month?		
b. Does some mastery testing facilitate the review of material covered several weeks previously?		
c. Is the mastery testing capable of diagnosing specific skill deficits in individual students?		
d. Are the mastery testing results being used to guide reteaching?		

Skill 5. Homework
Homework is managed appropriately.

Evaluation Questions	Rating and Notes	
a. Does the homework serve to consolidate skills already taught?		
b. Is the student error rate low?		
c. Is the homework corrected promptly?		
d. Is the homework highly aligned with daily lessons?		

D. Information Gathering: Teaching Functions

This section includes instruments that may be used to gather information on teaching functions in your classroom. The first instrument, "Analyzing Instructional Presentations," can be used to analyze the teaching functions you include in your daily lessons. The second instrument, "The Review Game," will help you set up and monitor daily, weekly, and monthly reviews in your classroom. The third instrument, "Speaking Clearly and Fluently," will assist you in analyzing your verbal presentations and interactions in the classroom. Directions for using the instruments are included.

Analyzing Instructional Presentations

Analyzing your instructional presentations will help you discover which of the effective teaching functions you include in your daily lessons. Generally, these functions include daily reviews, prerequisite checks, structured presentations of new content, guided practice, independent practice, diagnostic reviews, and mastery testing. Using a tape recorder with a counter, please tape-record one of your academic classes and then use the Instructional Presentation Analysis Form (Form 3.1b) to analyze the class session.

In the first column on the Instructional Presentation Analysis Form, fill in the teaching functions as they occur during the class session (see the code at the bottom of the form, and filled-in sample Form 3.1a). In the second and third columns, fill in the respective beginning and ending counter numbers. For example, the lesson might begin with a daily review (DR) that starts at counter number 0001 and ends at counter number 0300. Feel free to make any notes in the column provided, to help you remember the specific activity you engaged in.

Name **Brad A.**   Date **3/28/88**
Class **Math**   Page **1** of **1**

Instructional Presentation Analysis Form

Teaching Function*	Beginning Counter #	Ending Counter #	Notes:
DR	0001	0100	Pacing seemed a little slow
NP	0110	0470	Double-digit multiplication
GP	0523	1000	Presented 10 examples
IP	1100	1500	Ran short on time - Had to go to lunch - no summary

* DR= Daily Review, PC= Prerequisite Check, NP= New Presentation, GP= Guided Practice, IP= Independent Practice, DIR= Diagnostic Review, MT= Mastery Testing

Name _____   **Date** _____

Class _____   **Page** _____ **of** _____

Instructional Presentation Analysis Form

Teaching Function*	Beginning Counter #	Ending Counter #	Notes:

* DR= Daily Review, PC= Prerequisite Check, NP= New Presentation, GP= Guided Practice, IP= Independent Practice, DIR= Diagnostic Review, MT= Mastery Testing

Establish a set of review cards for one subject area, using the model shown as Form 3.2. It is recommended that you have two or three questions or problems for each objective. Use the Review Monitoring Form (Form 3.3b) to keep track of group progress on daily, weekly, and monthly reviews. In the column labeled "Type of Review," circle D for daily, W for weekly, and M for monthly reviews. (See the completed sample, Form 3.3a.) In the column labled "Notes," record comments about students who may need reteaching.

FORM 3.2   Model Review Card

Review Card

Subject Area: Grade:

Objective:

Reference:

Questions or Problems:

(Write the correct response on the reverse side)

Review Monitoring Form

Date	Type of Review*			# of Items	# Items Correct	Notes:
3/28	(D)	W	M	5	4	Reviewed facts about constellations.
	D	W	M			
	D	W	M			
4/28	D	W	(M)	50	37	Reviewed facts about constellations again. Students need more daily and weekly review.
	D	W	M			
	D	W	M			
	D	W	M			
	D	W	M			
5/1	(D)	W	M	5	3	
5/2	(D)	W	M	5	4	
5/3	(D)	W	M	5	5	Improvement noted!
5/4	(D)	W	M	5	5	
	D	W	M			
	D	W	M			
	D	W	M			
	D	W	M			
	D	W	M			
	D	W	M			
	D	W	M			
	D	W	M			
	D	W	M			
	D	W	M			
	D	W	M			
	D	W	M			
	D	W	M			
	D	W	M			
	D	W	M			
	D	W	M			
	D	W	M			

* D= Daily, W= Weekly, M= Monthly   (Circle One)

Review Monitoring Form

Date	Type of Review*			# of Items	# Items Correct	Notes:
	D	W	M			
	D	W	M			
	D	W	M			
	D	W	M			
	D	W	M			
	D	W	M			
	D	W	M			
	D	W	M			
	D	W	M			
	D	W	M			
	D	W	M			
	D	W	M			
	D	W	M			
	D	W	M			
	D	W	M			
	D	W	M			
	D	W	M			
	D	W	M			
	D	W	M			
	D	W	M			
	D	W	M			
	D	W	M			
	D	W	M			
	D	W	M			
	D	W	M			
	D	W	M			
	D	W	M			
	D	W	M			
	D	W	M			
	D	W	M			

* D= Daily, W= Weekly, M= Monthly   (Circle One)

Analyzing your instructional presentations will help you discover how clearly and fluently you speak. Using a tape recorder, please tape-record one of your academic classes (for example, a reading class). Then use the analysis form (Form 3.4) to examine your manner of speaking. Place a tally mark in the appropriate box in the portion labeled "Frequency Count," each time you hear yourself use an approximation, an indeterminate term, or an ambiguous expression. Also write a brief note about the particular expression that you used, in the appropriate box in the portion labeled "Expressions Used." This exercise will help you become aware of the manner in which you speak. Following the exercise, you may want to concentrate on eliminating and replacing some expressions you habitually use. Repeating the exercise at a later date will provide feedback about the changes you have made in your verbal presentations.

Name_____   Date_____

Class_____

Speaking Clearly and Fluently
How Well Did I Do?

Approximations: "Almost, Pretty much, About as"

Frequency Count:

Expressions Used:

Indeterminate Terms: "A bunch, A couple, Few, Some"

Frequency Count:

Expressions Used:

Ambiguous Expressions: "All of this, Somewhere, Other people"

Frequency Count:

Expressions Used:

E. Practical Suggestions: Teaching Functions

The practical suggestions in this section represent a collection of ideas based on classroom observations, experience, and a review of the effective teaching literature and teacher magazines. Feel free to incorporate any of the suggestions that work for you.

Daily, Weekly, and Monthly Reviews

a. General Reviews.
  (1) Review student grades frequently.
  (2) Ask questions about concepts or skills taught in previous lessons.
  (3) Give short quizzes.
  (4) Have students correct each other's homework.
  (5) Have students prepare a short written summary of previous work.
  (6) Plan "warm-up" activities, such as a three-minute math timing on facts.

b. Schedule Reviews.
  (1) Schedule reviews at the end of each unit.
  (2) Schedule reviews on a weekly and monthly basis.
  (3) Establish a "bank" of items that can be included in regularly scheduled reviews.

Presentation of New Content

a. Introduce the Purpose of the Lesson.
  (1) Explain to students the purpose or goal that you hope to accomplish in a given lesson.
  (2) Provide students with a rationale about the relevance of the purpose or goal of the lesson.
  (3) Relate the new information that you are going to introduce to previous information the student currently knows.
  (4) Help students understand how the new information relates to their own lives.

b. Introduce the Specific Order of the Lesson.
  (1) Present the specific order the lesson will follow.
  (2) Outline the content of the lesson for the students.
  (3) Write the outline on the blackboard or overhead projector; check off the items as they are covered.

c. Introduce Successive Topics or Tasks in a Lesson.

    (1) After you have covered the first topic in a lecture, give students a warning that you are going to move on to the next topic.

    (2) Before presenting a new step in a lesson, make sure students have been adequately prepared for it by a previous step.

d. Avoid Approximations and Ambiguous Expressions.

    (1) Avoid using approximations such as "almost," "pretty much," and "about as."

    (2) Avoid using indeterminate terms such as "a bunch," "a couple," "few," and "some."

    (3) Avoid using ambiguous expressions such as "all of this," "other people," and "somewhere."

    (4) Avoid overusing utterances such as "uh" and "um."

    (5) Monitor your use of such terms by videotaping or tape-recording your classroom presentations.

    (6) Make a list of approximations you currently use, and next to each approximation, write a better way of phrasing your idea.

e. Use a Clear, Confident Voice.

    (1) Express yourself in a pleasant, confident manner.

    (2) Make sure you can be easily heard.

    (3) Use inflections in your voice to facilitate understanding and maintain attention.

    (4) Check whether the level of your speech pattern is appropriate for your students.

f. Present Lessons Using a Three-step Process.

    (1) Effective instruction can be introduced in a three-step process:

        (a) Teacher demonstrates the correct response.

        (b) Teacher prompts students to perform the correct response with the teacher.

        (c) Students practice the correct response.

    (2) With younger students, you might present these three steps by saying

        (a) My turn . . .

        (b) Our turn . . .

        (c) Your turn . . .

g. Summarizing Methods.

    (1) Ask questions at the end of an instructional presentation to determine the extent to which students understood what was covered.

    (2) Pose problems to the students; have them work out solutions applying the information they have learned.

    (3) Use the same sorts of techniques that are appropriate for reviewing information.

h. Present Clear Summaries.

    (1) Vary your summaries. They can be composed of teacher-talk, or they can invoke student participation.

    (2) Use your outline of the lesson to help in pulling together a summary. This is a great form of review.

    (3) Don't do your summaries impromptu. Use your outline of the lesson and rephrase the main points.

    (4) Make certain to highlight any points that students were confused about during the presentation.

    (5) Ask yourself what information you most want students to remember. Keep the amount of information appropriate for the level on which students are working.

    (6) Avoid abrupt endings.

    (7) Reduce the level of difficulty rather than slow the pace.

    (8) Set the stage for the next learning activity.

Guided Student Practice

a. Present Sufficient Examples.

    (1) Have several examples ready in case some students have difficulty relating to the first ones you use.

    (2) Make certain that your examples are closely related to the topic or task.

    (3) Use concrete examples, especially with the more difficult concepts. That is, the more difficult the concept, the more concrete the examples need to be initially.

    (4) Move from the simple to the complex.

    (5) When initially presenting a concept, use positive examples rather than nonexamples.

b. Set Guidelines for Determining Success.

    (1) When making decisions about how successfully students are handling tasks, observe their performance and involvement in terms of the learning objectives.

    (2) Make certain at least 80 percent of your students can complete at least 80 percent of tasks assigned to them during the allotted time.

    (3) During guided practice, make certain that success rates are around 80 percent.

c. Address Low Mastery Rates.

(1) Check to make certain the students don't consistently have low success rates (below 65 percent), which suggest that the teacher is "teaching over the students' heads" or has not prepared them effectively for the questions.

(2) Develop alternatives for use when students have problems. For example, develop one alternative to use when students are not quite getting the skill (e.g., demonstration). Develop a second alternative for use when some students are not quite getting the skill although others appear to have it (e.g., ask a skilled student to demonstrate).

(3) Develop a third alternative for use when students are not even close to performing correctly (e.g., have the students go back and work on prerequisite skills).

Independent Student Practice

a. Set Guidelines for Determining Success.

(1) During independent work, success rates are between 90 and 100 percent. The success rate during independent work must be higher than that attained during guided practice, because the teacher is not available to provide assistance.

(2) Use the independent practice time to provide further guided practice for students still needing additional assistance.

F. Self-improvement Plan: Teaching Functions

After completing the self-evaluation checklist (Section C) and reading through the practical suggestions (Section E), you should be prepared to develop a self-improvement plan (SIP). Please complete portion A, entitled "Teaching Functions: Goals and Objectives," on the self-improvement plan, by checking the goal(s) and objective(s) you wish to include in your plan. Also, write a brief narrative describing how you plan to address the requirements in portions B–E. Complete portion F, "Results," after you have completed your self-improvement project. (See Chapter 2, Section F, for a completed self-improvement plan).

Self-improvement Plan: Teaching Functions

Name _____ Class _____ Date _____

A. Teaching Functions: Goals and Objectives
   1. Daily, Weekly, and Monthly Reviews
      a. General reviews.
      b. Schedule reviews.
      c. Other _____
   2. Presentation of New Content
      a. Introduce the purpose of the lesson.
      b. Introduce the specific order of the lesson.
      c. Introduce successive topics or tasks in a lesson.
      d. Avoid approximations and ambiguous expressions.
      e. Use a clear, confident voice.
      f. Present lessons using a three-step process.
      g. Summarizing methods.
      h. Present clear summaries.
      i. Other _____
   3. Guided Student Practice
      a. Present sufficient examples.
      b. Set guidelines for determining success.
      c. Address low mastery rates.
      d. Other _____
   4. Independent Practice
      a. Set guidelines for determining success.
      b. Other _____
B. Practical Suggestions
   Please indicate which of the practical suggestions from Section E you plan to use to meet each of the objectives. (You may include practical suggestions from other sources as well.)
C. Specific Procedures
   Please describe the specific procedures you will use to implement the practical suggestion(s).
D. Current and Desired Performance
   Please describe your current performance and desired performance in regard to each of the objectives you have selected. You may state the performance in terms of student behavior, such as student mastery rates.

E. Timelines and Change Measures

Please describe your timelines and how you will measure change in relationship to the objective(s) you have selected.

F. Results

Upon completion of your self-improvement project, write a brief description of the results of its implementation. Attach any raw data sheets that were used to gather information and describe any changes that were made during your project.

References

Block, J.H. (1980). Success rate. In C. Denham & A. Lieberman (Eds.), *Time to learn* (pp. 95–106). Washington, D.C.: U.S. Department of Education, National Institute of Education.

Brophy, J. (1987). *Research linking teacher behavior to student achievement: Potential implications for instruction of Chapter I students.* Unpublished manuscript. Michigan State University, East Lansing, Mich.

Copeland, W.D. (1987). Classroom management and student teachers' cognitive abilities: A relationship. *American Educational Research Journal, 24*(20), 219–236.

Doyle, W. (1985). Effective secondary classroom practices. In R.M.J. Kyle (Ed.), *Reading for excellence: An effective schools sourcebook.* Washington, D.C.: U.S. Government Printing Office.

Evertson, C., Emmer, E.T., & Brophy, J.E. (1980). Predictors of effective teaching in junior high mathematics classrooms. *Journal of Research in Mathematics Education, 11,* 167–178.

Fisher, C.W., Berliner, D.C., Filby, N.N., Marliave, R., Cahen, L.S., & Dishaw, M.M. (1980). Teaching behaviors, academic learning time, and student achievement: An overview. In C. Denham & A. Lieberman (Eds.), *Time to learn* (pp. 7–32). Washington, D.C.: U.S. Department of Education, National Institute of Education.

Gagne, R. (1970). *The conditions of learning.* New York: Holt, Rinehart and Winston.

Good, T.L., & Grouws, D.A. (1979). The Missouri mathematics effectiveness project. *Journal of Educational Psychology, 71* 355–362.

Good, T.L., Grouws, D.A., & Ebmeier, H. (1983). *Active mathematics teaching.* (Research on Teaching monograph series.) New York: Longman.

Hunter, M. (1984). Knowing, teaching, and supervising. In P.L. Hosford (Ed.), *Using what we know about teaching* (pp. 169–193). Alexandria, Va.: Association for Supervision and Curriculum Development.

Hunter, M., & Russell, D. (1981). Planning for effective instruction: Lesson design. *Increasing your teaching effectiveness.* Palo Alto, Calif.: Learning Institute.

Lightfoot, S.L. (1983). *The good high school: Portraits of character and culture.* New York: Basic Books.

Noli, P. (1980). A principal implements BTES. In C. Denham & A. Lieberman (Eds.), *Time to learn* (pp. 213–222). Washington, D.C.: U.S. Department of Education, National Institute of Education.

Rosenshine, B., & Stevens, R. (1986). Teaching functions. In M.C. Wittrock (Ed.), *Handbook of research on teaching,* 3rd ed. (pp. 376–391). New York: Macmillan.

Samuels, S.J. (1981). Some essentials of decoding. *Exceptional Education Quarterly, 2,* 11–25.

Voelker Morsink, C., Chase Thomas, C., & Smith-Davis, J. (1987). Noncategorical special education programs: Process and outcomes. In M.C. Wang, M.C. Reynolds, & H.J. Walberg (Eds.), *Handbook of special education: Research and practice* (pp. 287–311). New York: Pergamon Press.

CHAPTER 4

Academic Feedback

A. The Research Literature
   Academic Feedback Concepts
   Academic Feedback and Independent Practice
   Expectations, Participation, and Feedback
B. Knowledge Quiz: Academic Feedback
   Answer Key: Knowledge Quiz (Academic Feedback)
C. Self-evaluation Checklist: Academic Feedback
   Instructions for Completing the Self-evaluation
      Checklist
   Self-evaluation Checklist
D. Information Gathering: Academic Feedback
   Analyzing Questions
   Analyzing Feedback
E. Practical Suggestions: Academic Feedback
   Question Types
   Delivering the Questions
   Reactions to Student Responses
F. Self-improvement Plan: Academic Feedback
References

A. The Research Literature

The term *academic feedback* refers to those procedures a teacher uses to provide students with information on the accuracy of their oral or written responses to academic questions. Academic feedback is "strongly and consistently related to student achievement" (Filby & Cahen, 1985). The importance of academic feedback has been stressed by researchers studying effective teachers at all grade levels in all basic skills areas. Questions are one of the major vehicles for academic feedback. Brophy and Good (1986) reported that one of the differences between effective and less effective teachers was the frequency of questions. The effective teachers asked approximately three times as many questions as the less effective teachers.

In discussing the findings from a major study, the researchers (Fisher et al., 1980) made the following observation on the nature and importance of academic feedback:

> Many different specific behaviors fulfilled this function, including answering questions in class, checking papers, using programmed texts, and listening to oral reading. The percentage of instructional time during which the student received feedback was positively related to student engagement rate and to achievement [p. 20].

In investigating the behavior of effective elementary teachers, Stallings, Cory, Fairweather, and Needels (1977) noted that teachers of classes that made the greatest gains gave more instruction, asked more academic questions, and provided more feedback. In a study of junior high and high school teachers, Stallings, Cory, Fairweather, and Needels (1978) reported that the effective teachers provided more opportunities for academic responses, praised student successes, and provided support and corrective feedback when students did not respond correctly. In contrast, the less successful teachers spent less time interacting with students and more time in organizing rather than instructing.

In summarizing the findings from a series of studies, Brophy and Good (1986) made the following observation, stressing the importance of a strong academic orientation in interactions with students:

> . . . teachers who produced the most achievement were businesslike and task oriented. They enjoyed working with students but interacted with them primarily within a teacher-student relationship. They operated their classrooms as learning environments, spending most time on academic activities. Teachers who produced the least achievement usually showed either of two contrasting orientations. One was a heavily affective approach in

which the teachers were more concerned with personal relationships and affective objectives. The other (fortunately, least common) pattern was seen in disillusioned or bitter teachers who disliked their students and concentrated on authority and discipline in their interviews [p. 341].

Academic Feedback Concepts

Much of the research on academic feedback and effective teachers has stressed the importance of (a) feedback opportunities, (b) question types, (c) delivering the questions, and (d) reacting to student responses.

1. Feedback Opportunities.   If students are to receive extensive and appropriate academic feedback, a basic prerequisite is a strong emphasis on increasing the amount of academic instruction. It is possible for students to receive a large amount of feedback unrelated to instruction in a specific skill. Feedback on student misbehavior and feedback on nonacademic tasks are not positively correlated with increased achievement. Indeed, extensive feedback related to misconduct is usually correlated negatively with instructional effectiveness. Brophy and Good (1986) reported that a large amount of criticism for misconduct "almost invariably correlates negatively with achievement, and indicates classroom organization and management difficulties" (p. 338).

If the teacher is to create opportunities for academic feedback, consideration must be given to both increasing the amount of instructional time and structuring the academic instruction to facilitate academic feedback opportunities. If the academic instruction is presented in rather large steps and loosely supervised, the opportunity for academic feedback is limited. If the teacher presents information in small steps and intensively supervises the students, the opportunities for academic feedback are increased. Small steps mean that students are generating more academic responses per lesson. Intense supervision is important; teachers cannot provide feedback if they do not know what students are doing or where the students should be going academically.

In analyzing the practices of more effective teachers, Good, Grouws, and Ebmeier (1983) noted that they were far more likely to assign homework and far more likely to provide feedback on the homework. In discussing the attitudinal reactions of students, the researchers reported, "It would seem that the emphasis upon variables, like review and homework (when done in the context of meaningful and successful practice), does not necessarily lower attitudes, as it is sometimes argued" (p. 77).

In summary, because academic feedback is so closely integrated with other time management and instructional presentation skills, a decision to increase the amount of academic feedback could involve a wide range of changes. To increase the quality and quantity of academic feedback, the teacher must first create an environment in which academic feedback is an integral and important part of the teaching process. When academic feedback is associated with such important teaching functions as daily reviewing, guided practice, and reteaching, it is not just feedback to the student, but for the teacher as well. Student performance is a measure of instructional effectiveness, and higher error rates should signal the teacher to modify instructional procedures (see Figure 4.1).

2. Question Types.   A teacher's questions can be varied by such practices as changing the difficulty level, changing the cognitive level, and varying the clarity.

Question difficulty. There is a common trend in the level of difficulty of the question asked by effective teachers. Success rates tend to be in the 80 to 90 percent range for the more effective teachers, and in the 60 to 70 percent range for the less successful teachers (Brophy & Good, 1986). Rosenshine and Stevens (1986) summed up the issue of question difficulty with the recommendation quoted on the next page.

FIGURE 4.1

Feedback for Both Student and Teacher

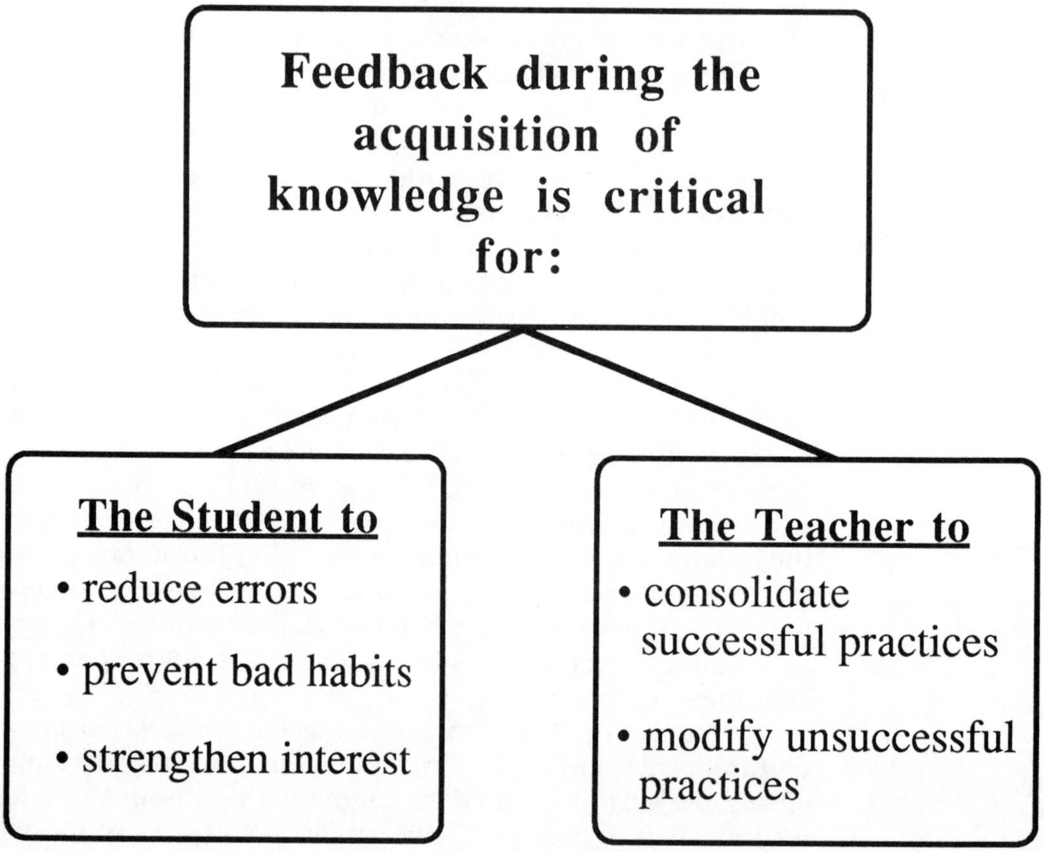

```
┌─────────────────────────────┐
│   Feedback during the       │
│    acquisition of           │
│  knowledge is critical      │
│         for:                │
└─────────────────────────────┘
        ╱              ╲
┌─────────────────┐  ┌──────────────────────┐
│ The Student to  │  │  The Teacher to      │
│                 │  │                      │
│ • reduce errors │  │ • consolidate        │
│                 │  │   successful practices│
│ • prevent bad   │  │                      │
│   habits        │  │ • modify unsuccessful│
│                 │  │   practices          │
│ • strengthen    │  │                      │
│   interest      │  │                      │
└─────────────────┘  └──────────────────────┘
```

The frequency of teacher questions is not the only important factor, because the precentage of correct student responses also plays a role in successful learning. The importance of a high percentage of rapid ("automatic"), correct responses is a relatively new idea resulting from recent research. Although there are not scientific guidelines as to exactly what the percentage of correct answers should be, a reasonable recommendation at the present time is an 80 percent success rate when practicing new material. When reviewing, the success rate should be very high, perhaps 90 percent, and the student reponses should be rapid, smooth, and confident [p. 383].

Cognitive level. The cognitive level of a question is usually treated separately from the difficulty level. It was once assumed that instruction would be more effective if the teacher's questions required the student to use more complex mental processes, such as inductive reasoning.

Low-level questions are typically "What?", "Where?", and "When?" questions. An example of a low-level question would be "What is the first step in adding decimal numbers?" High-level questions are typically "Why?" and "How?" questions. An example of a high-level question would be "How do we find the sale price if we know the discount?"

Although the research on cognitive levels contains inconsistencies, some conclusions can be stated with a reasonable level of confidence. Brophy and Good (1986) have listed the following observations, based on their review of the research:

The data do refute the simplistic (but frequently assumed) notion that higher-level questions are categorically better than lower-level questions. Several studies indicate that lower-level questions facilitate learning, even learning of higher-level objectives. Furthermore, even when the frequency of higher-level questions correlates positively with achievement, the absolute numbers on which these correlations are based typically show that only about 25 percent of the questions asked were classified as higher level. Thus, in general, we should expect teachers to ask more lower-level than higher-level questions, even when dealing with higher-level content and seeking to promote higher-level objectives [p. 363].

Question clarity. Brophy and Good (1986) wrote, "In general, clarity of presentation is one of the more consistent correlates of achievement" (p. 355). Clarity can be reduced if the teacher

a. Uses vague or ambiguous questions.
b. Uses disjointed questions, particularly ones that are interrupted by inserting additional background information.
c. Speaks too quietly or incoherently, or addresses the blackboard rather than the students.
d. Asks two or more questions without stopping to get an answer to the first one.
e. Fails to get student attention before posing the question.

3. Delivering the Questions.   Questions should facilitate student engagement in academic learning tasks. Questions should also serve to provide feedback to the teacher on the effectiveness of the instruction. A few well-placed questions will tell the teacher if reteaching is necessary. Teacher questions can be directed to groups or individuals.

In their summary of the research on effective questioning, Rosenshine and Stevens (1986) noted, "One technique for obtaining a high frequency of responses in a minimum amount of time is through group choral responses" (p. 384). For choral responding to be effective, the teacher has to use some type of signal to ensure that students respond at the same time. A consistent and briskly paced presentation style is a way of signaling students. Rosenshine and Stevens (1986) further noted, "Choral responses can be an effective way to conduct guided practice" (p. 385).

There appears to be considerable support for a questioning strategy that uses a combination of choral and individual responding. The choral responses are stressed in the earlier stages of guided practice; and individual responses are stressed in the latter stages, when the success rate is higher.

When using individual questions, care must be taken to pose the question before selecting a student. Care should also be taken to ensure that all students are equally involved in the questions. It is very common for a teacher to give the majority of questions to those few students who are eager to respond.

4. Reactions to Student Responses.   Rosenshine and Stevens (1986) have noted that most students' responses to questions can be grouped in four categories:

a. Correct, quick, and firm
b. Correct, but hesitant
c. Incorrect, but a careless error
d. Incorrect, suggesting lack of knowledge of facts or a process

Correct and firm responses. When the student answer is correct and confident, the instructor should not break the momentum with a lengthy statement or extensive praise. A quick "Right" and the presentation of the next question should follow a correct and highly confident student response.

Correct and hesitant responses. If the student is in the initial stages of learning and gives a correct but hesitant response, the teacher should take the time to praise the student for the correct response and review the reasons for the correct answer or the steps associated with finding the correct answer. This quick review will be particularly important if the teacher feels that there are other class members who are also in the initial stages of learning the skill.

Incorrect and careless responses. When the student makes a careless error, the teacher should respond with a quick and simple correction and allow the student to provide the correct answer. The student should not be berated, but the teacher's feedback should make it clear to the student and the whole class what the correct answer should be. The feedback need not provide the reasons why the answer is correct.

Incorrect due to lack of knowledge. If the student's response indicates that the student lacks knowledge of the facts or procedures necessary to arrive at the correct answer, Rosenshine and Stevens (1986) suggested two options:

1. Provide the students with prompts or hints to lead them to the correct answer.
2. Reteach the material to the students who do not understand [p. 385].

They further noted: "Both of these approaches to error correction—that is, prompting and reteaching—have been used successfully in experimental research and in effective instructional programs" (p. 385).

Reteaching and prompting in response to a student's demonstrated lack of knowledge is sometimes termed a *correction procedure.* The quality of a teacher's correction procedures reflects the quality of all procedures used to present new content. If the teacher is not providing students with elegant rules and practical problem-solving strategies, such rules and strategies will not be available to use in correction procedures for specific errors. Indicators that a teacher may not be providing students with elegant rules and practical problem-solving strategies would include the use of correction procedures characterized by inconsistent responses to different students for the same error, long and convoluted explanations, or explanations that add nothing but tension (e.g., "You wouldn't give a stupid answer if you were thinking").

A correction procedure should, where possible, finish with the student supplying the correct answer. Such a procedure should leave the student with dignity intact.

Questions, dignity, and momentum. As the more effective teachers present new content, they use briskly paced, question-packed, attention-demanding presentations, with a student success rate of 80 percent or better on written problems and oral questions. To ensure continued student involvement, there must be a large number of questions and high rate of success. To preserve both the instructional momentum and individual student dignity, a teacher needs a systematic set of strategies for preventing and dealing with student errors in responding to questions. The previously listed suggestions for responding to different correct and incorrect student responses should be supplemented with a range of strategies to prevent errors, maintain momentum, and protect student dignity.

One of the best error-prevention procedures involves careful rehearsal of questions with choral responses and targeted individual questions. Choral responses are an excellent vehicle for questions and feedback without threatening individual egos. If the choral responses are followed by individual questions, to higher-performing students first and then to lower-performing students, the probability of success will be higher.

If a student makes an error, quickly rephrase the question with additional prompting and a reduced level of difficulty. Do not prolong this correction process, or you will lose instructional momentum and add to student embarrassment. You should plan to review the question later on in the lesson, also to return to that student with a question that he or she can answer (see Figure 4.2).

Psychological climates for errors. One of the more difficult aspects of giving feedback to students who have made errors relates to the importance of creating a classroom climate where errors are a natural part of the learning process rather than "sins" to be taken personally by teacher or student. Some teachers are reluctant to give feedback on the academic errors for fear of "hurting the student's feelings." Such an approach indicates that the teacher has not created a healthy climate for dealing with errors.

Some teachers will help create a healthy climate by deliberately making errors themselves so that they can model appropriate reactions and demonstrate that there is nothing morally wrong with errors. These deliberate errors are usually made when students have demonstrated high levels of mastery. At such time, the probability of students detecting the error is high, and the risk of student confusion is low. Few things increase student interest more than the possibility of detecting a teacher error.

The teacher who reacts defensively to a student's identification of a teacher error creates a punishing environment for feedback. The teacher who praises a student for detecting a teacher error creates a healthy climate for feedback. Nothing is more destructive to group activities than the presence of individuals who react defensively to feedback. The teacher who models appropriate reactions to feedback from students will be teaching an invaluable social survival skill of lifelong value.

Regardless of what procedures are used, teachers should systematically work for a psychological climate in which feedback to students and from students can be given directly and honestly without the risk of "hurt feelings."

Academic Feedback and Independent Practice

Fisher et al. (1980) noted that a high frequency of "explanation specifically in response to student need" was negatively related to student achievement. They reported that the presence of extensive individual feedback during seatwork may be an indicator that the instruction has structural deficits. This would certainly be the case if students were prematurely placed in independent practice. Fisher et al. (1980) made the following observation with regard to a high frequency of explanation in response to student

FIGURE 4.2

Questions and Errors

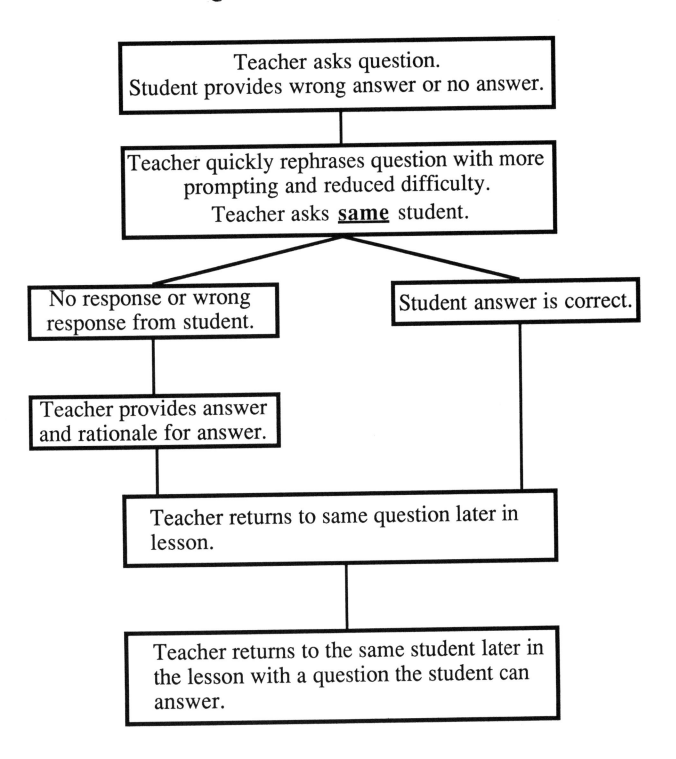

need during seatwork: "Frequent need for explanation may be a signal that changes are needed in the student's instructional program, either in the difficulty of the assignments or in preparation for seatwork" (p. 21).

A Dilemma.   Filby and Cahen (1985) noted that feedback is "one aspect of a basic teacher's dilemma." They described the dilemma as follows:

> A teacher can maximize instructional contact by having whole-class instruction. However, this means that the same content must be taught to all students at the same time. If the class is heterogeneous in terms of skill levels or instructional needs, whole-class instruction may mean inappropriate instructional content for some students. . . . In pursuit of appropriate instruction to meet individual needs, a teacher may establish groups in the classroom. Grouping immediately increases the complexity of the management tasks and is likely to decrease student attention [p. 213].

The fact that whole-class instruction tends to be more highly correlated with student achievement than the more individualized settings is testimony to the importance of the cycle of presentation, monitoring, and feedback—as well as the fact that it is facilitated in group settings.

If a teacher understands that some instructional functions are more easily supported in group and individual settings, serious management errors can be prevented. A serious error occurs when a teacher fails to exploit the strength of a setting or fails to minimize the weakness of a setting. For example, the teacher who talks excessively and fails to question extensively during whole-class instruction does not take advantage of the opportunity for extensive feedback present in the whole-class setting. The teacher that has all students working on exactly the same task during individual seatwork (e.g., independent practice on the same problem) is not using the strength of that setting and adjusting learning tasks to individual needs. In the latter case, the students lose in two ways, because the tasks may be inappropriate and the feedback limited. The teacher, who initiates small-group instruction without the extensive preparation and clear instructions needed to reduce management problems, will negate strengths of the small-group setting (see Figure 4.3).

The whole-class setting is a difficult one if the teacher wishes to vary the task content for different learners. However, it is well suited to providing the needed range of student learning experiences—new content presentation, guided practice, and independent practice. In individual settings, the reverse is true. It is easier to vary the content of learning tasks but very difficult to provide the needed range of learning experiences. Too often the student will not receive the needed guided practice and feedback because of the management problems associated with the individual in-

FIGURE 4.3 Appropriate Tasks and Feedback: A Dilemma

Instructional Setting	Feedback Potential	Management	Appropriate-ness of Tasks
Whole Class	Extensive opportunities	Easiest	Difficult for content Easy for experience
Small Group	Moderate opportunities	Difficult	Moderate difficulties for content Moderate difficulties for experience
Individual Seatwork	Limited opportunities	Difficult to do right	Easy for content Difficult for experience

structional setting. For a learning task to be appropriate, both the content and the learning experience have to be appropriate. For example, a learning task might consist of guided practice (the learning experience) on multiplication problems with one-place decimals and two-digit numbers (the task content).

One of the advantages of using group instruction first and finishing a class with individual seatwork (as shown in Table 3.1 of Chapter 3) is the teacher's increased capacity to monitor students during the first part of the lesson to determine which ones should be receiving guided practice on problem areas during the individual seatwork. The most effective teachers using whole-class instruction will maximize opportunities for feedback and conduct timely, well-targeted reteaching to reduce student errors and minimize the individual differences in knowledge deficits.

Practice and Feedback. Berliner and Fisher (1985) stated that "Practice, by itself, is not always the best way to learn a complex skill" (p. 336). This will certainly apply if students receive extensive unsuccessful independent practice. If only extensive practice were needed, then college faculty would have more legible handwriting than upper elementary students. Every master teacher of the early elementary grades is aware that a small amount of carefully supervised handwriting practice, with extensive feedback on all the complex processes involved, is far more effective than large amounts of loosely supervised practice. Loosely supervised handwriting practice in the early grades will generate poor habits that will handicap individuals for the rest of their lives.

Some third-grade teachers can teach time telling to one-minute intervals in two weeks; others take all year. One of the key differences lies in the intensity and quality of the practice and associated feedback. The master teacher will select one method (e.g., the 2:45 method) and teach it to mastery. The teacher may even contact parents to ensure that students receive no conflicting feedback (e.g., by using the 15 till 3:00 method) during the critical skill-acquisition period.

In the early stages of teaching word problems, the student will need feedback on the accuracy of the answer and feedback on the quality of the problem-solving strategies used to arrive at the answer. The more complex the task and the earlier the stage of knowledge acquisition, the more sensitive, targeted, and intensive the feedback must be. Proficiency in this complex aspect of the teaching craft has important implications for increased attitudinal and achievement outcomes in students and reduced remedial workloads for the teacher.

Expectations, Participation, and Feedback

The use of effective academic feedback procedures helps create high expectations for all students. It has been noted that "Teachers who set and communicate high expectations to all their students obtain greater academic performance than teachers who set low expectations" (U.S. Department of Education, 1986, p. 32).

Indicators that low expectations have been established for certain students include:

a. Students are seated father away from the teacher.
b. Students receive less direct instruction.
c. Students have fewer opportunities to learn new material.
d. Students are asked to do less work.
e. Teachers call on these students less often.

The academic feedback procedures are an important component in an integrated set of procedures. The level of implementation of the feedback procedures reflects the degree to which a teacher has mastered the total set of integrated procedures and the degree to which the teacher is committed to meeting the needs of all students.

B. Knowledge Quiz: Academic Feedback

Multiple Choice

Question 1 Research has shown that effective teachers

a. ask as many questions as less effective teachers.
b. ask 10 percent more questions than less effective teachers.
c. ask 150 percent more questions than less effective teachers.
d. ask 300 percent more questions than less effective teachers.

Question 2 A firm, correct response by a student should be followed by

a. extensive praise and quick movement to the next question.
b. prompting or reteaching.
c. a short confirmation and quick movement to the next question.
d. a praise statement and quick review of the reasons why the answer was correct.

Question 3 A hesitant, correct response by a student should be followed by

a. extensive praise and quick movement to the next question.
b. prompting and reteaching.
c. a short praise statement and quick movement to the next question,
d. a praise statement and a quick review of the reasons the answer was correct.

Question 4 If using a combination of choral and individual responses,

a. stress individual responses in the initial stages of learning.
b. stress choral responses in the initial stages of learning.
c. use choral responses only with independent practice.
d. use choral responses only with guided practice.

Question 5 For questions to be effective,

a. all questions should be "high-level" questions.
b. the majority of the questions should be "high-level" questions.
c. "high-level" questions can be in the minority.
d. "low-level" questions can be in the minority.

Question 6 *Academic feedback* refers to

a. questions only.
b. teachers' oral feedback on academic issues.
c. academic tests.
d. a range of written and oral interactions between teacher and student.

Question 7 An effective correction procedure is often characterized by

a. reteaching and prompting.
b. a teacher response to student misbehavior.
c. teaching students to correct other students.
d. inconsistent responses to different students for the same error.

Question 8 Students seated farther away and receiving less direct instruction often

a. are the most independent students.
b. are the most successful students.
c. have low teacher expectations.
d. have high teacher expectations.

Question 9 The use of elegant rules and practical problem-solving strategies facilitates

a. effective correction procedures.
b. students' errors.
c. confusion in low achievers.
d. long explanations.

Question 10 "What," "where," and "when" questions would be characterized as

a. high-level questions.
b. low-level questions.
c. difficult questions.
d. easy questions.

Fill in the Blanks

Question 11 A teacher asks a question. The student response is incorrect. The teacher rephrases the question and simplifies it. The student response is incorrect. What does the teacher do next?

What else should the teacher do before the end of the lesson?

a.

b.

Question 12 With individual seatwork, it is reasonably easy to vary the _____ for each student, but more difficult to provide the needed range of _____ _____ _____, such as new content presentation and guided practice.

Question 13 In the whole-class setting, it is easier to provide the range of _____ _____ _____, but more difficult to vary the _____.

Question 14
Management is _____ in small-group settings and _____ in whole-class settings.

Question 15
Feedback opportunities are often _____ in individual seatwork.

Answer Key: Knowledge Quiz (Academic Feedback)

Multiple Choice

Question 1   Research has shown that effective teachers

d. ask 300 percent more questions than less effective teachers.

Question 2   A firm, correct response by a student should be followed by

c. a short confirmation and quick movement to the next question.

Question 3   A hesitant, correct reponse by a student should be followed by

d. a praise statement and a quick review of the reasons the answer was correct.

Question 4   If using a combination of choral and individual responses,

b. stress choral responses in the initial stages of learning.

Question 5   For questions to be effective,

c. "high-level" questions can be in the minority.

Question 6   *Academic feedback* refers to

d. a range of written and oral interactions between teacher and student.

Question 7   An effective correction procedure is often characterized by

a. reteaching and prompting.

Question 8   Students seated farther away and receiving less direct instruction often

c. have low teacher expectations.

Question 9   The use of elegant rules and practical problem-solving strategies facilitates

a. effective correction procedures.

Question 10   "What," "where," and "when" questions would be characterized as

b. low-level questions.

Fill in the Blanks

Question 11 A teacher asks a question. The student response is incorrect. The teacher rephrases the question and simplifies it. The student response is incorrect. What does the teacher do next? *The teacher provides the answer and a rationale for the answer.* What else should the teacher do before the end of the lesson?

a. *The teacher should return to the same question later in the lesson.*

b. *The teacher should return to the same student later in the lesson with a question that he or she can answer.*

Question 12
With individual seatwork, it is reasonably easy to vary the *content* for each student, but more difficult to provide the needed range of *student learning experiences*, such as new content presentation and guided practice.

Question 13
In the whole-class setting, it is easier to provide the range of *student learning experiences*, but more difficult to vary the *content*.

Question 14
Management is *difficult* in small-group settings and *easier* in whole-class settings.

Question 15
Feedback opportunities are often *limited* in individual seatwork.

C. Self-evaluation Checklist: Academic Feedback

.Instructions for Completing the Self-evaluation Checklist

The self-evaluation checklist on the following pages should be completed using the following scale and criteria.

1 = No change is needed in present practices.

2 = There are minor problems that can be corrected quickly and easily.

3 = There are major problems that will require a considerable investment in time and effort.

4 = I need more specific information on my own behavior before I can decide whether I have a problem.

The evaluation questions are provided as a guide to the type of specific behaviors that exemplify each of the effective teaching skills. You should feel free to add evaluation questions if you feel that they will increase the practicality and sensitivity of the evaluation process. In many cases, extra space has been provided to allow for added evaluation questions.

Please make supporting notes that will help describe any problems in more detail. Notes should address the context; for example, certain problems may be more or less noticeable, depending on the time, the class, the individual student, the lesson activity, and the subject being taught.

If the space provided on the evaluation checklist is not sufficient, supplement the checklist by adding descriptive material and cross-referencing supplementary material with the number of the skill and the letter of the evaluation question (e.g., Skill 2, Question c).

Additional information on the criteria and the use of the self-evaluation checklist is provided in Section C of Chapter 2.

Self-evaluation Checklist

Skill 1. Feedback Opportunities
A classroom environment has been created that provides for extensive academic interactions between teacher and students.

Evaluation Questions		Rating and Notes
a. Have procedures been used to ensure that a large amount of time is allocated to academic instruction?		
b. Do lessons include appropriate amounts of guided practice and daily reviews?		
c. Is new material presented in small steps with large amounts of academic feedback?		
d. Depending on content, are appropriate amounts of oral and written feedback used?		

Skill 2. Questioning
The questions are consistent with the instructional needs.

Evaluation Questions		Rating and Notes
a. Are student success rates appropriate for the lesson activity?		
b. Do the questions support the presentation of new content in small steps?		
c. Are questions to individuals posed before the individual is named?		
d. Do questioning procedures maintain instructional momentum?		

Rating Scale: 1 - No change; 2 - Minor problems; 3 - Major problems; 4 - Insufficient information

Skill 3. Student Responses
Individual responses, group responses, and written responses are used to ensure high levels of involvement from all students.

Evaluation Questions		Rating and Notes
a. Is the teacher blending choral and individual responses where their use is appropriate?		
b. Are all the students being equally involved during individual questioning?		
c. When appropriate does the teacher require written responses to the most important skills?		

Skill 4. Reacting to Student Responses
Teacher reactions are consistent with student responses to questions.

Evaluation Questions		Rating and Notes
a. Does the hesitant, correct response typically receive stronger praise and a quick review?		
b. For incorrect responses for lack of knowledge, does the teacher rephrase the question or reteach?		
c. Do correction procedures indicate the use of elegant rules and practical problem-solving strategies?		
d. Do teacher's responses to student errors indicate an atmosphere where students are not afraid to make errors?		

Skill 5. Question Clarity
Questions are clearly framed and clearly delivered.

Evaluation Questions		Rating and Notes
a. Are questions short and precise, or rambling and disjointed?		
b. Are questions delivered clearly and audibly?		
c. Are questions clearly aligned with the content focus of the lesson?		
d. Is student attention gained before questions are posed?		

D. Information Gathering: Academic Feedback

This section includes two forms that may be used to gather information on academic feedback activities in your classroom: Form 4.1 to help you analyze the questions you ask during class presentations, and Form 4.2 to collect information about the manner in which students respond to your questions.

Analyzing Questions

Form 4.1 is designed to help you analyze the type of questions you ask in your classroom. (See the completed sample, Form 4.1a.) You will need to tape-record a class session and then analyze the types of questions using the blank form (Form 4.1b).

Form 4.1, "Analyzing Questions," addresses three categories: type of question, difficulty of the question, and nature of the required response. You should code each question that you asked during the class session by circling the appropriate option under each heading on Form 4.1b.

If the question is coded as "content," the other two categories should also be coded. However, if the type of question is "organize" (organizational) or "noncontent," one of the other two categories may not apply. In such a case, please leave the inapplicable categories blank, as shown in Form 4.1a.

Whenever more than one question in a row is asked of the same student, after coding each question, bracket the questions asked of that student (see Form 4.1a).

Question Categories.*

1. Type of Question
    a. Content
        (1) Lesson-oriented questions
        (2) Concerned with specific lesson content
        (3) Student response required
        (4) Examples: Whom did Mary visit? What is the vowel in the word "rat"?

*From *Effective Teaching for Successful Mainstreaming* by Barbara Larrivee. Copyright © 1985 by Longman, Inc. Reprinted by permission of Longman, Inc.

b. Organizational

    (1) Concerned with classroom procedures

    (2) Primarily management-oriented

    (3) Student's response not evaluated

    (4) Examples: Does anyone need help? How many have finished the worksheet?

c. Noncontent

    (1) Not related to lesson

    (2) Primarily personal reference

    (3) Nonthreatening questions to students about how and what they are doing

    (4) Solicitation of comments by teacher

    (5) Requests by teacher for student question

    (6) Examples: How many of you like pizza? John, do you have any sisters?

2. Cognitive (Difficulty) Level

  a. Low cognitive level

    (1) What? Where? When?

    (2) Drill questions (usually fast-paced)

    (3) Answer available from information previously given or read

    (4) Examples: What is 7 times 6? Who is the president of the United States?

  b. High cognitive level

    (1) Questions that stimulate thinking (Why? How?)

    (2) Questions that require students to seek explanations, reason, translate, interpret, and solve problems

    (3) Examples: Why do you think the dog ran away? What effect did John's leaving have on the group?

3. Response Required

  a. Narrow response required

    (1) Predictable response

    (2) Specific right or wrong answer

    (3) Response choice limited

    (4) Examples: Who can tell me the vowel in "rock"? What happened to Jane's doll?

  b. Open response required

    (1) Unpredictable response

    (2) Many responses acceptable

    (3) Examples: Can someone use "quick" in a sentence? If you were Jack, what would you have done?

FORM 4.1a

Name _Joe F._

Class _Science_

Date _1/26/88_

Analyzing Questions

Type of Question	Cognitive Level	Response Required	Notes:
(Content) Organize Noncontent	High (Low)	(Narrow) Open	Who invented the telescope?
Content Organize Noncontent	High Low	Narrow Open	
Content (Organize) Noncontent	High (Low)	Narrow (Open)	Where is your work?
Content (Organize) Noncontent	High (Low)	(Narrow) Open	Do you have it finished?
(Content) Organize Noncontent	High (Low)	(Narrow) Open	When was the telescope
Content Organize Noncontent	High Low	Narrow Open	invented?
Content Organize (Noncontent)	High (Low)	(Narrow) Open	What time is it?
Content Organize Noncontent	High Low	Narrow Open	
Content Organize Noncontent	High Low	Narrow Open	
Content Organize Noncontent	High Low	Narrow Open	
Content Organize Noncontent	High Low	Narrow Open	
Content Organize Noncontent	High Low	Narrow Open	
Content Organize Noncontent	High Low	Narrow Open	
Content Organize Noncontent	High Low	Narrow Open	
Content Organize Noncontent	High Low	Narrow Open	
Content Organize Noncontent	High Low	Narrow Open	
Content Organize Noncontent	High Low	Narrow Open	
Content Organize Noncontent	High Low	Narrow Open	
Content Organize Noncontent	High Low	Narrow Open	
Content Organize Noncontent	High Low	Narrow Open	
Content Organize Noncontent	High Low	Narrow Open	
Content Organize Noncontent	High Low	Narrow Open	
Content Organize Noncontent	High Low	Narrow Open	
Content Organize Noncontent	High Low	Narrow Open	
Content Organize Noncontent	High Low	Narrow Open	
Content Organize Noncontent	High Low	Narrow Open	

Tony (bracketed beside rows 3–5)

Name _____

Date _____

Class _____

Analyzing Questions

Type of Question	Cognitive Level	Response Required	Notes:
Content Organize Noncontent	High Low	Narrow Open	
Content Organize Noncontent	High Low	Narrow Open	
Content Organize Noncontent	High Low	Narrow Open	
Content Organize Noncontent	High Low	Narrow Open	
Content Organize Noncontent	High Low	Narrow Open	
Content Organize Noncontent	High Low	Narrow Open	
Content Organize Noncontent	High Low	Narrow Open	
Content Organize Noncontent	High Low	Narrow Open	
Content Organize Noncontent	High Low	Narrow Open	
Content Organize Noncontent	High Low	Narrow Open	
Content Organize Noncontent	High Low	Narrow Open	
Content Organize Noncontent	High Low	Narrow Open	
Content Organize Noncontent	High Low	Narrow Open	
Content Organize Noncontent	High Low	Narrow Open	
Content Organize Noncontent	High Low	Narrow Open	
Content Organize Noncontent	High Low	Narrow Open	
Content Organize Noncontent	High Low	Narrow Open	
Content Organize Noncontent	High Low	Narrow Open	
Content Organize Noncontent	High Low	Narrow Open	
Content Organize Noncontent	High Low	Narrow Open	
Content Organize Noncontent	High Low	Narrow Open	
Content Organize Noncontent	High Low	Narrow Open	
Content Organize Noncontent	High Low	Narrow Open	
Content Organize Noncontent	High Low	Narrow Open	
Content Organize Noncontent	High Low	Narrow Open	
Content Organize Noncontent	High Low	Narrow Open	
Content Organize Noncontent	High Low	Narrow Open	

Analyzing Feedback

In order to analyze the feedback you provide to students in academic situations, tape-record a class session. Use Form 4.2b, "Academic Feedback: Data Collection Form." In filling it out, follow the example of the partially completed sample, Form 4.2a. The left column is for noting each question you asked. The columns in the middle are for indicating whether the question was asked of the group or of an individual and how the student(s) responded to the questions. The right-hand column is for notes about how you reacted to the response(s).

Academic Feedback
Data Collection Form

Name *Judy S.* Date *3/18/88*

Feedback Opportunities (Notes about Questions)	Questions		*Student Responses				** Teacher Reactions Notes
	Grp	Indiv	1	2	3	4	
Jim, What's 3x3?		✓		✓			Right! 3x3 is 9
What's 6x7?	✓		✓				(go to next fact)
What's 9x9, Don?	✓					✓	If we had nine groups of 9 each, how many would we have? (Draw tally marks)

* Student Responses: 1 =Correct & Firm, 2 =Correct but Hesitant, 3 =Incorrect & Careless, 4 = Incorrect but doesn't know

** Examples of Teacher Reactions Quick Affirmation, Move on to Next Question, Praise Correct Response, Review Reasons for Correct Response, Quick and Simple Correction, Move on, Clarify Correct Response for Class, Prompt Correct Answer, Reteach Concept

Academic Feedback

Data Collection Form

Name _____   Date_____

Feedback Opportunities (Notes about Questions)	Questions		*Student Responses				** Teacher Reactions Notes
	Grp	Indiv	1	2	3	4	

* **Student Responses:** 1 =Correct & Firm, 2 =Correct but Hesitant, 3 =Incorrect & Careless, 4 = Incorrect but doesn't know

** **Examples of Teacher Reactions**   Quick Affirmation, Move on to Next Question, Praise Correct Response, Review Reasons for Correct Response, Quick and Simple Correction, Move on, Clarify Correct Response for Class, Prompt Correct Answer, Reteach Concept

E. Practical Suggestions: Academic Feedback

The practical suggestions in this section represent a collection of ideas based on classroom observations, experience, and a review of the effective teaching literature and teacher journals. Feel free to incorporate any of the suggestions that work for you.

Question Types

a. Difficulty Level of Questions.
    (1) Check to see that at least 75 percent of the questions you ask elicit correct responses.
    (2) Check to see that the other 25 percent of the questions you ask elicit some type of response (incorrect or incomplete). Be alert to situations where students fail to respond at all.
    (3) Ask more low-order questions (Who, What, When, Where). Lower-order questions facilitate learning, even learning of higher-level objectives (Why).
    (4) Concentrate on academic content; don't overdo questions about personal experiences.
    (5) Design recitation questions to help students encode and remember recently presented information. Design discussion questions to induce students to process information at higher cognitive levels (application, analysis, synthesis, evaluation). Design review and drill questions to prepare students for tests or to verify that they have mastered the material.

b. Clarity of Questions.
    (1) Ask questions one at a time.
    (2) Check to make certain that the students understand the questions you ask.
    (3) Ask a large number of questions, and keep the questions simple.
    (4) Ask some questions in an ordered-turn fashion. This procedure ensures that all students will have opportunities to participate, and it simplifies group management. Keep a copy of your class list handy; check off names as questions are asked of individual students. Make notes about students who need help.
    (5) Organize questions in a sequence that is designed to accomplish some particular instructional purpose. Questions should not be asked in a haphazard manner.

Delivering the Questions

a. Wait for Students to Answer.

  (1) Be sensitive to the length of time you wait for a response from a student after asking a question. The length of the time you should wait depends on the difficulty of the question being asked.

  (2) For a drill-and-practice type of question, the response time should be one second or less.

  (3) For a question at a higher cognitive level, you may need to wait three to five seconds in order to give the students time to process the question and think about answering it.

  (4) Make sure that your questions have a maximum impact in terms of stimulating the students to think about the content. Address your questions to the class as a whole; that is, do not single out one individual.

b. Guidelines for Using Criticism.

  (1) Use correction, not criticism.

  (2) When correcting, focus on academic content; don't confront the student personally.

  (3) Make sure that only about 1 percent of your feedback is criticism.

  (4) Specify the desired alternative behavior. Tell students what you want them to do.

c. Increasing Praise.

  (1) Everyone knows that a little praise goes a long way in any classroom, but "a little praise" needs to be more than the same few phrases repeated over and over, ad nauseam. Your students need more than the traditional "Good," "Very good," and "Fine" if encouragement is in the card. Here are some additional possibilities:*

That's very nice	For sure
Wow!	That's amazing
I like the way you're working	Keep up the good work
	Much better
That's a big improvement	It's a pleasure to teach when you work like this
Keep it up	You really outdid yourself today
Good job	
What neat work	Congratulations. You earned 100 percent today
This kind of work pleases me very much	Terrific
That's right! Good for you	Beautiful

*Adapted from E.S. Kubany, Sixty-five Ways to Say "Good for You," *Teacher,* September 1972, pp. 8–10.

I bet your parents would be proud to see the job you did on this

Excellent work

Very good. Why don't you show the class?

Marvelous

Groovy

Absolutely right

That looks like it's going to be a great report

You're on the right track now

John is in line

Dickie got right down to work

It looks like you put a lot of work into this

Very interesting

That's an interesting way of looking at it

That's the right answer

Exactly right

Superior work

That's a very good observation

Thanks for raising your hand, Charles. What is it?

Out of sight

Far out

That's coming along nicely

I'm very proud of the way you worked today

I appreciate your help

Thank you for (sitting down, being quiet, getting right to work, etc.)

Rad

Sharp

I like the way Tom is working

My goodness, how impressive!

That's "A" work

Mary is waiting quietly

Ann is paying attention

That's clever

Very creative

Good thinking

Now you've figured it out

Clifford has it

Now you've got the hang of it

Super

That's a good point

That's an interesting point of view

You're really concentrating

You've got it now

Nice going

You make it look easy

I like the way Bill (the class) has settled down

Reactions to Student Responses

a. Feedback for Quick, Firm, Correct Responses.

(1) Recognize a correct response with a brief remark such as "Yes," "That's right," or "Correct."

(2) Maintain the momentum of practice sessions. Move on to the next question or flashcard after a correct answer.

(3) Don't elaborate on correct responses.

(4) Repeat answers as a form of acknowledgment.

(5) Provide quick, firm, correct responses during the later stages of learning or in a review.

b. Feedback for Correct but Hesitant Responses.

   (1) Provide short statements of feedback, such as ''Correct,'' or ''Very good,'' during initial stages of learning (i.e., guided practice).

   (2) Explain the steps a student used to arrive at the correct answer. Doing so should help other students understand the answer as well.

   (3) Tailor the instructional feedback that you provide to the type of oral response made by the student.

c. Feedback for Incorrect Responses Due to Lack of Knowledge.

   (1) Rephrase the question. Provide clues to the answer. Give the student more time to figure out the answer.

   (2) Help the student figure out the answer rather than calling on another student to answer the question.

   (3) Don't merely say, ''No'' or ''That's wrong.'' Explain why a student's answer is wrong. Help students see what step in the process they missed. Point out the steps they did correctly.

   (4) Don't give the correct answer immediately.

d. Feedback for Failing to Respond Due to Lack of Knowledge.

   (1) Train students to use a phrase such as ''I don't know,'' rather than not responding at all.

   (2) After waiting for a short period of time, ask the student, ''Do you know?'' This should serve as a prompt for using the statement, ''I don't know.''

   (3) If students frequently fail to respond, it may be necessary to reteach a particular concept.

   (4) Use different-colored ink pens to record grades in your gradebook. By doing so, you can quickly see how well the group or individual student is doing.

   (5) Keep contacts brief—thirty seconds or less. Contacts of longer duration are detrimental, because the teacher loses the attention of the rest of the group.

   (6) Provide remedial instruction during recess, lunch, art, music, physical education, or before or after school.

   (7) Correct errors early in instruction, because it often becomes more difficult to correct later, and it interferes with learning new information.

F. Self-improvement Plan: Academic Feedback

After completing the self-evaluation checklist (Section C) and reading through the practical suggestions (Section E), you should be prepared to develop a self-improvement plan (SIP). Please complete portion A, entitled "Academic Feedback: Goals and Objectives," on the self-improvement plan, by checking the goal(s) and objective(s) you wish to include in your plan. Also, write a brief narrative describing how you plan to address the requirements in portions B–E. Complete portion F, "Results," after you have completed your self-improvement implementation project. (See Chapter 2, Section F, for a completed self-improvement plan).

Self-improvement Plan: Academic Feedback

Name _____ Class _____ Date _____

A. Academic Feedback: Goals and Objectives
  1. Feedback Opportunities
     a. In-class feedback.
     b. Out-of-class feedback.
     c. Other _____
  2. Question Types
     a. Difficulty levels of questions.
     b. Clarity of questions.
     c. Other _____
  3. Deliver the Questions
     a. Wait for students to answer.
     b. Guidelines for using criticism.
     c. Increasing praise.
     d. Other _____
  4. Reactions to Student Responses
     a. Feedback for quick, firm, correct responses.
     b. Feedback for correct but hesitant responses.
     c. Feedback for incorrect responses due to lack of knowledge.
     d. Feedback for failing to respond due to lack of knowledge.
     e. Other _____

B. Practical Suggestions
   Please indicate which of the practical suggestions from Section E you plan to use to meet each of the objectives. (You may include practical suggestions from other sources as well.)

C. Specific Procedures
   Please describe the specific procedures you will use to implement the practical suggestion(s).

D. Current and Desired Performance
   Please describe your current performance and desired performance in regard to each of the objectives you have selected. You may state the performance in terms of student behavior, such as frequency of student firm, correct responses.

E. Timelines and Change Measures
   Please describe your timelines and how you will measure change in relationship to the objective(s) you have selected.

F. Results

Upon completion of your self-improvement project, please submit copies of this form and a brief description of the results of its implementation. Attach any raw data sheets that were used to gather information and describe any changes that were made during your project.

References

Berliner, D.C., & Fisher, C.W. (1985). One more time. In D.C. Berliner & C.W. Fisher (Eds.), *Perspectives on instructional time* (pp. 333–347). (Research on Teaching monograph series.) New York: Longman.

Brophy, J., & Good, T. (1986). Teacher behavior and student achievement. In M.C. Wittrock (Ed.), *Handbook of research on teaching*, 3rd ed. (pp. 328–375). New York: Macmillan.

Filby, N.N., & Cahen, L.S. (1985). Teacher accessibility and student attention. In C.W. Fisher & D.C. Berliner (Eds.), *Perspectives on instructional time* (pp. 203–214). (Research on Teaching monograph series.) New York: Longman.

Fisher, C.W., Berliner, D.C., Filby, N.N., Marliave, R., Cahen, L.S., & Dishaw, M.M. (1980). Teaching behaviors, academic learning time, and student achievement: An overview. In C. Denham & A. Lieberman (Eds.), *Time to learn* (pp. 7–32). Washington, D.C.: U.S. Department of Education, National Institute of Education.

Good, T.L., Grouws, D.A., & Ebmeier, H. (1983). *Active mathematics teaching.* (Research on Teaching monograph series.) New York: Longman.

Kubany, E.S. (1972, September). Sixty-five ways to say "Good for you." *Teacher*, 8–10.

Larrivee, B. (1985). *Effective teaching for successful mainstreaming.* New York: Longman Publishing.

Rosenshine, B., & Stevens, R. (1986). Teaching functions. In M.C. Wittrock (Ed.), *Handbook of research on teaching*, 3rd ed. (pp. 376–391). New York: Macmillan.

Stallings, J., Cory, R., Fairweather, J., & Needels, M. (1977). *Early childhood education classroom evaluation.* Menlo Park, Calif.: SRI International.

————. (1978). *A study of basic reading skills taught in secondary schools.* Menlo Park, Calif.: SRI International.

U.S. Department of Education. (1986). *What works?* Washington, D.C.: U.S. Department of Education.

CHAPTER 5

Academic Monitoring

A. The Research Literature
   Academic Monitoring Concepts
B. Knowledge Quiz: Academic Monitoring
   Answer Key: Knowledge Quiz (Academic Monitoring)
C. Self-evaluation Checklist: Academic Monitoring
   Instructions for Completing the Self-evaluation
      Checklist
   Self-evaluation Checklist
D. Information Gathering: Academic Monitoring
   The Academic Monitoring Form
   Interaction Monitoring
E. Practical Suggestions: Academic Monitoring
   Monitoring and Goals
   Providing for Timely Monitoring
   Decision Making and Corrective Action
   Monitoring and the Improvement of Instruction
F. Self-improvement Plan: Academic Monitoring
References

A. The Research Literature

Brophy and Good (1986) made the following observation on the importance and complexity of the teaching role:

> Elitist critics often undervalue teaching, or even suggest that anyone can teach. ("Those who can, do; those who can't, teach.") The data reviewed here refute this myth as well. Although it may be true that most adults could survive in the classroom, it is not true that most could teach effectively. Even trained and experienced teachers vary widely in how they organize the classroom and present instruction. Specifically, they differ in several respects: (a) the expectations and achievement objectives they hold for themselves, their classes, and individual students; (b) how they select and design academic tasks, and (c) how actively they instruct and communicate with students about academic tasks. Those who do these things successfully produce significantly more achievement than those who do not, but doing them successfully demands a blend of knowledge, energy, motivation, communication and decision-making skills that many teachers, let alone ordinary adults, do not possess [p. 370].

The decision-making skill that Brophy and Good referred to clearly distinguishes between effective and ineffective teachers. Effective teachers make instructional decisions that adjust instruction based on the needs and performance of their students, whereas ineffective teachers present instructional material on a random or a rigid, prescheduled basis and fail to adjust for student performance. Such instructional practices are devoid of the decision-making skills that ensure that instructional practices will be progressively improved.

Rosenshine and Stevens (1986) noted that most teachers (including unsuccessful ones) employ teaching practices that could help them make appropriate decisions—for instance, daily reviews and guided student practice. The successful teachers use the information they gather while implementing these practices to make decisions. In addition, they do so more frequently and at more appropriate times than less successful teachers. Making appropriate instructional decisions requires knowing what to do and when to do it. Such decision making requires constant monitoring of student performance.

The research literature on the qualities of effective teaching leaves no doubt on this issue: The effective teacher is a manager and decision maker who continually monitors the class and adjusts instruction based on student performance.

In discussing "expert classroom management," Brophy and Good (1986) made the following observations:

(a) They [teachers] demonstrated "withitness" by monitoring the entire class when they were instructing, and by moving around during seatwork time.

(b) What these teachers demanded, however, was not so much compliance with authority as productive engagement in academic activities, and

(c) Students were accountable for careful, complete work, because they knew that the work would be checked and followed up with additional instruction or assignments if necessary [p. 341].

Thus, for teachers to be effective decision makers, they must meet the following important requirements:

a. They must know what instructional practices are appropriate for different situations.

b. They must always be aware of the situation at hand, so that they can implement appropriate instructional alternatives.

To meet these requirements, teachers must employ a range of different academic monitoring skills. Specifically, teachers need monitoring skills to keep them aware of such factors as

a. The students' immediate reactions to instructional practices during a lesson

b. The extent to which each student is progressing toward the long-term instructional goals of the course

c. The extent to which different instructional practices help students achieve their long-term educational objectives

The effective teaching literature has documented the relationship between the teacher's academic monitoring skills and the relationship with student achievement. In one study, the researchers (Fisher et al., 1980) reported their findings as follows:

Teachers were asked to predict how their students would do on certain test items used in the achievement battery. This accuracy in predicting student performance was used as a measure of the teacher's diagnostic ability. A positive relationship was found between a teacher's diagnostic ability and the reading and math achievement of students [p. 19].

Academic Monitoring Concepts

1. Monitoring and Goals. The two major purposes of academic monitoring are closely related: the attainment of student goals and the progressive improvement of instructional practices.

Rosenshine (1979), in identifying the critical aspects of successful instruction, recommended that teachers set clear instructional goals and monitor student progress toward those goals. In addition, teachers must set and maintain clear, firm, and reasonable work standards. Students must know exactly what is expected in completing an assignment, how the format of the assignment should look, how neat the work should be, and the accuracy level they are expected to attain. If teachers establish objective standards, they will be more able to evaluate student performance.

When teachers hold students accountable for completing work on time and for meeting standards, students will realize that the work they are doing has an important academic purpose. Likewise, parents can help in holding their children responsible for appropriately completing work. Teachers must solicit the assistance of parents in providing an appropriate environment at home so that students can successfully complete homework assignments. Teachers can provide parents with tips on how to support and reinforce classroom learning.

Before teachers can effectively monitor student progress, they must have in place a sequence of valid instructional objectives. To be instructionally valid, the sequence of objectives must be integrated with a validated instructional program. That is, the instructional objectives students are expected to meet should be a part of an instructional program that has been sufficiently tested. The program should be supported by data showing that similar students achieved high levels of mastery under similar conditions.

2. Instructional Programs and Embedded Progress Tests. To monitor student progress through a sequence of specific instructional objectives, instructional programs generally provide embedded progress tests. It is critical that instructional programs include tests that are instructionally diagnostic, are sensitive to changes in student performance, and provide for timely monitoring activities.

Instructionally diagnostic. The cross-referencing between specific items on the progress tests and the corresponding lessons of the instructional programs should be readily apparent. Consequently, there should be a high degree of correspondence between what is being tested and what is being taught.

Sensitivity to student change. Progress tests must be sensitive to changes in student performance. Tests must have the power to detect changes, if they exist, and clearly point out areas where students are having difficulties. Sensitive tests will quickly alert teachers to specific decisions they must make in planning future instruction.

Providing for timely monitoring. Progress tests should be scheduled in such a way that they provide for the timely monitoring of student progress. Testing should be conducted frequently enough to ensure that a student with a substantial skill deficit is quickly noticed. For example, when there is daily instruction in basic skills, comprehensive weekly testing will usually be required along with daily checks on the content covered in each lesson.

Instructional programs that are instructionally diagnostic, are sensitive to changes in student performance, and provide for timely monitoring will produce many benefits for both students and teachers.

Benefits to students. Instructional programs with high-quality monitoring programs are very helpful in developing positive student attitudes. Consistent demonstrations of success are among the most important ingredients in any approach to attitude development. For example, weekly tests should give students a sense of accomplishment and a sense of movement through the curriculum.

Timely, sensitive monitoring and the associated reteaching will increase student success. The importance of such success was stressed in one comprehensive study of elementary classroom practices. The researchers (Fisher et al., 1980) reported as follows:

> It is interesting to note that the high success component of learning is associated with more positive student attitudes. Successful students probably enjoy learning more because of their success. Failure, even when it is only occasional, appears to result in a more negative attitude among elementary school students [p. 24].

Benefits to teachers. High-quality monitoring programs can also help teachers maintain enthusiasm. Obviously, effective teaching is not always easy, and teachers need to be reminded that their hard work is making a difference. Reviewing monitoring data should remind teachers of their effectiveness and value.

3. Decision-making and Corrective Action.

Monitoring practices should be designed so that they naturally facilitate corrective actions. For example, a monitoring program should quickly give a teacher information about those students who are prepared to move ahead, those students who are not prepared, those students who have made careless errors, and those students who require reteaching of a particular concept. Next, based on this type of monitoring information, a process for providing corrective actions must be built into the system. If reteaching is not systematically planned, it may not occur. One simple way to plan for reteaching is to schedule one daily lesson per week in which no new material is taught. The lesson can be used for diagnostic mastery testing and reteaching, dictated by the results of the mastery testing. If mastery testing indicates that some students have a major problem, the teacher should not hesitate to delay the instruction of new material until mastery of the earlier material has been achieved.

Reteaching and misbehavior. Teachers should avoid using testing and reteaching as punishment. It is important that teachers react positively to the necessity for testing and any associated reteaching. Such statements as "The tests show you have not been working, so we will keep repeating this material until you learn to pay attention" imply that reteaching is being used as a punishment for student misbehavior.

For the most part, student skill deficits can be explained as either a student learning problem or a teaching problem. Good, Grouws, and Ebmeier (1983), in a description of teachers of students who made higher gains than those of other teachers, stated that these teachers "assumed partial responsibility for student learning and appeared to be ready to reteach where necessary" (p. 61).

4. Monitoring and the Improvement of Instruction.   The second purpose for instructional monitoring involves the improvement of instruction. Many school districts place an emphasis on the collection of data on student progress. The huge banks of standardized test data that exist in many school districts may or may not achieve their potential as agents for change. In some cases, the process of the data collection becomes an end in itself. The data has no instructional value if it is not used to guide the progressive improvement of instruction. In some cases, data is collected for the primary purpose of classifying students or teachers as high or low achievers. The teacher who views the data collected on student progress as primarily for the purpose of classifying the student as an A, B, C, D, or F student is also suggesting that it is the student and not the instruction that must change. Such an attitude is not conducive to the progressive improvement of instruction. Such a teacher might have difficulty with a school administrator who uses the information on teaching performance for the classification of the teacher as effective or ineffective only. It is to be hoped that the supervisor would place the primary emphasis on supporting teachers in their efforts to improve their instruction (see Figure 5.1).

Good, Grouws, and Ebmeier (1983) observed that effective teachers considered it particularly important "to look for ways to confirm or disconfirm that their presentations had been comprehended by students" (p. 61).

Verifying comprehension. In verifying comprehension, teachers must study the elements of an instructional lesson. Elements such as daily reviews, the presentation of new content, guided practice, and independent practice bear a dynamic and dependent relationship to each other. To implement such elements effectively, the teacher monitors student performance to determine the appropriate timing and relative emphasis to place on each element.

Teachers must make two timing decisions that are critical to successful instruction. They must decide

a. When to move from the daily review and prerequisite check to the introduction of new content

b. When to move from guided practice to independent practice.

Frequent and well-timed academic monitoring is needed to make these decisions.

FIGURE 5.1

The Purpose of Monitoring

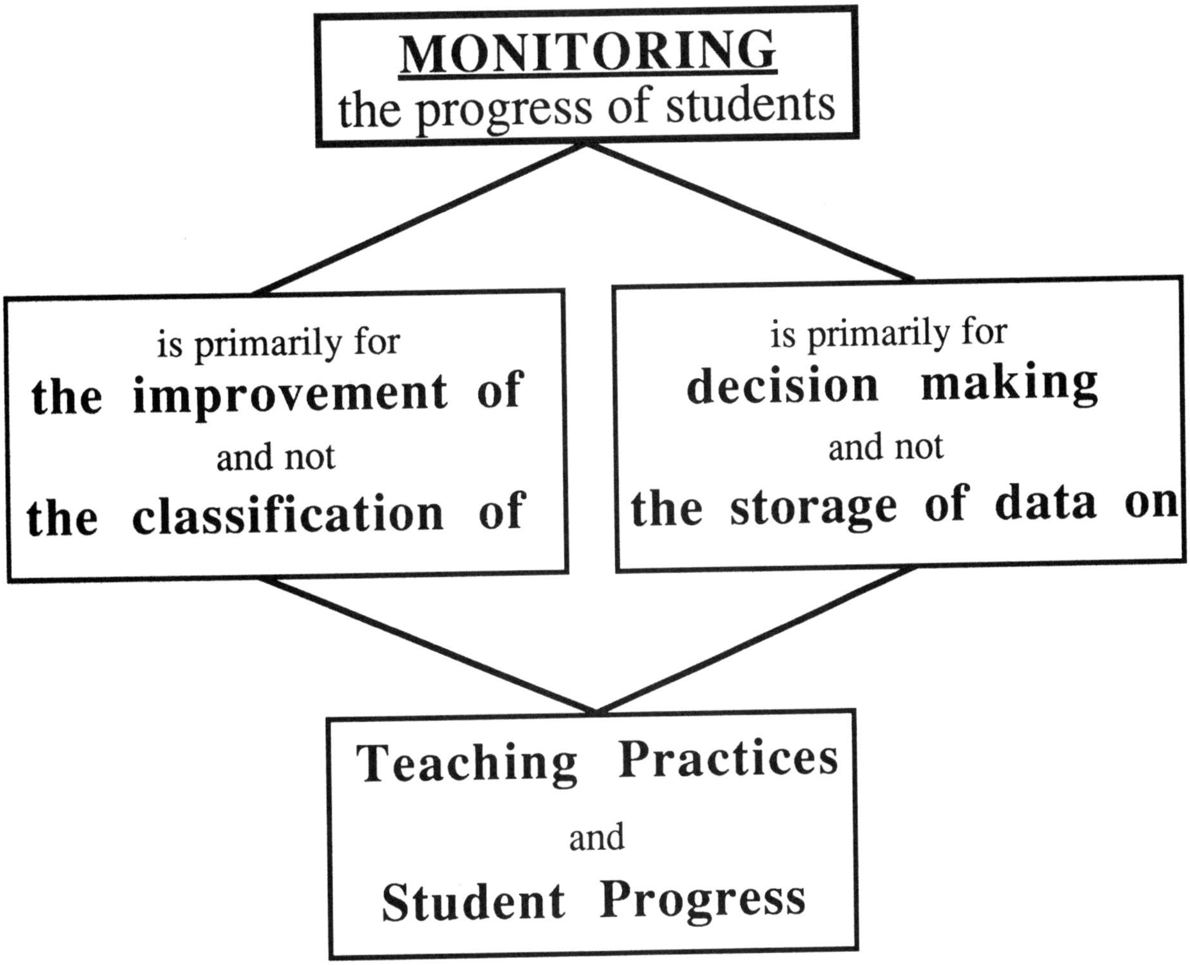

```
┌─────────────────────────────────┐
│        MONITORING               │
│    the progress of students     │
└─────────────────────────────────┘
```

┌──────────────────────────┐   ┌──────────────────────────┐
│   is primarily for   │   │   is primarily for   │
│   **the improvement of** │   │   **decision making**   │
│   and not   │   │   and not   │
│ **the classification of**│   │ **the storage of data on**│
└──────────────────────────┘   └──────────────────────────┘

┌──────────────────────────┐
│   **Teaching   Practices**│
│   and   │
│   **Student Progress** │
└──────────────────────────┘

Premature presentations of new content. One of the most common reasons for student failure is the premature presentation of new content. If a student needs a prerequisite skill to be successful in a new skill, all the student motivation and instructor sincerity in the world will not help the student. For instance, the teaching of long division without first ensuring that the students "overlearn" subtraction skills would be an exercise in student frustration and instructional incompetency. Unless a teacher closely monitors student performance on prerequisite skills, he or she will not know if the presentation of a new skill is premature.

Premature movement to independent practice. When students are assigned independent practice on objectives for which their error rate is high, the damage to student attitude and student achievement is also high. To assign material for which the student's success rate is less than 80 percent is to risk consolidation of bad habits, reduction in student confidence, and failure in future content. In addition, when teachers have to spend an inordinate amount of time remediating, the time available to present new material is significantly reduced. Also, if teachers assign homework that is too difficult for the students, the teacher's credibility is threatened as parents struggle to do what they feel the teacher should have done. Careful monitoring of student performance in guided practice will help ensure that independent practice consolidates skills and helps students consistently demonstrate success.

A caution for improving instruction: Circulate. All too frequently, teachers just provide assistance to students who ask for help or who volunteer to show them their work. Teachers should spend a high percentage of the time circulating around the room to check *all* students' performance, being especially sensitive to those students who don't ask questions but who still need help. Along with monitoring student progress, circulating will help increase on-task behavior and decrease disruptive behavior.

5. Instructional Alignment. The term *instructional alignment* refers to the alignment among the curriculum, the instructional activities, and the curriculum-embedded tests of student progress. Cohen (1987) observed that large instructional gains are possible when the curriculum, the instruction, and the measures of student progress are aligned. Such alignment facilitates

a. Increased instructional efficiency, because instructional activities are clearly focused
b. Student gains, because of the clear relationship between teacher effort and student outcomes
c. Positive student attitudes, because students are more likely to react positively to instruction that demonstrates a clear and consistent relationship between student investment in instruction and student test results

"The more complex and difficult the instructional tasks, the more important the role of alignment. Also, for low achievers, a little alignment goes a long way" (Cohen, 1987, p. 18).

6. Adaptive Ability. As schools try to meet the needs of a more diverse group of learners, the monitoring and decision-making skills of the teacher become more important. One of the greatest challenges facing educators is the creation of classroom environments with the ability to adapt instruction to meet the needs of all learners.

At one time, educators attempted to handle diversity in learners through the use of additional segregated treatment settings. Special-education, remedial, "disadvantaged," and other student populations were placed in separate programs, with specialists as instructors. Such practices generated the following concerns:

a. Many efficacy studies did not show these segregated, expensive education treatments to be more effective.

b. Although many of the segregated treatments were said to be justified on the basis that the student would receive needed and highly specialized services, there was considerable research to suggest that effective programs for most of the mildly handicapped students and effective programs for regular classrooms were more similar than different (Bickel & Bickel, 1986). Brophy (1987) reported that "research has turned up very little evidence suggesting the need for qualitatively different forms of instruction for students who differ in aptitude, achievement level, socioeconomic status, ethnicity, or learning style" (p. VI-122).

c. Serious questions were raised about the ethics associated with many of the approaches to program segregation, and federal laws were enacted to give preference to the regular classroom as the "least restrictive alternative."

d. Questions were raised about the long-term value of removing and segregating students as the preferred method of dealing with instructional problems. Such student removals implied that the student, not the instruction, was always at fault. Some observers even went so far as to suggest that schools were, in essence, "blaming the victim."

e. Because there developed a habit of removing even mildly handicapped special education students rather than modifying instructional practices, some felt that schools had lost the adaptive ability to handle other students "at risk," with problems such as those associated with cultural and linguistic diversity, drug abuse, teenage pregnancy, and teenage suicide. These concerns were heightened when it was revealed that dropout rates of 50 percent were not unusual in many schools and that the dropout phenomenon had broad impact on all ethnic and social class subgroups (Hahn, 1987).

Although there is nothing in the literature suggesting that phenomena such as the dropout epidemic are tied to a single issue or corrected by a single treatment, there certainly are researchers who stress the importance of effective teaching. In discussing the most effective treatments for dropouts, Hahn (1987) noted that these programs "challenged students academically and provided personal counseling and were staffed by caring adults." Hahn also noted that these programs "share some of the characteristics documented in the effective schools literature" (p. 261).

While the issues are important, difficult, and complex, there can be little doubt about the following facts:

a. More and more teachers will be asked to work with more students classified as "at risk."

b. One of the critical elements in the prevention and treatment of "at risk" students is the presence of the characteristics of effective instruction.

c. Adaptive instructional treatments can only be triggered in a timely manner if the teacher is effectively monitoring the progress of all students. Such monitoring should reflect the presence of a skillful instructor and a caring professional educator.

d. To date, the research on effective instructional treatments for diverse student populations suggests that the partial implementation of a wide and exotic range of instructional procedures has yielded less than the consistent and appropriate implementation of the academically focused instructional skills identified in the effective teaching literature.

7. Mastery Testing. Mastery testing is one component of a model of school learning described by Bloom (1968). In this model, student progress is monitored carefully. A students' advancement through the system of instruction requires the mastery of previous units before moving on. In their review of the research on mastery testing, Kulik and Kulik (1987) made the following observations:

a. Mastery testing generally has positive effects on student learning, and its value is well documented.

b. "Mastery testing raised the final examination average in the typical study by .54 standard deviations, or from the fiftieth to the seventy-first percentile" (p. 339).

c. "The effects of mastery testing were more apparent, however, on the low-aptitude students in a class than they were on the high-aptitude students. Thus, a mastery testing requirement also had the effect of diminishing individual differences in student achievement" (p. 339).

d. Mastery testing can be effective in group-based instruction and in more individualized instructional settings.

e. The effectiveness of mastery-based testing is increased when the amount of feedback on mastery tests is increased.

f. The effectiveness of mastery testing is related to the rigor with which it is implemented. Those who use high levels of mastery (e.g., 90 percent or better), and who ensure that a large percentage of the students achieve this before moving to new content, will do better than those who accept lower performance levels.

In many ways the intent of mastery learning is similar to that of ALT (academic learning time). Both stress the importance of large amounts of engaged time with high success levels. Both make the point that moderate levels of success are unacceptable for low or high aptitude students and that continued exposure to moderate levels of success has no positive correlation with increased academic performance. Both use a similar definition of success. For mastery testing, it is typically 90 percent or better, with the most effective programs using success levels of 95 or 100 percent. For ALT, the preferred level is 100 percent, except for careless errors. Careless errors are defined as errors that typically would not be repeated if the problem were repeated. For most practical purposes, the mastery testing definition and the ALT definition of success fall in the same range of 90 percent or better.

The intent of mastery learning is also similar to systematic reviewing and reteaching. If one is providing weekly quizzes, reteaching, and retesting until most students are achieving 90 percent or better, then one is conducting mastery testing.

Mastery testing appears to be consistently associated with the more effective instructional programs. One of the reasons for this may be the additional accountability that is generated by mastery testing. If students are tested and moved on to new content regardless of the test results, the teacher is under no pressure to examine or revise instructional practices. If reteaching is conducted until students reach an acceptable level of mastery before moving to new content, there is constant pressure to examine and revise instruction.

B. Knowledge Quiz: Academic Monitoring

Multiple Choice

Question 1 The term *instructionally diagnostic* refers to

a. use of diagnostic normative tests.
b. use of standardized tests.
c. the cross-referencing between test items and instructional elements.
d. the cross-referencing between curriculum and instructional elements.

Question 2 Monitoring is conducted to

a. grade students.
b. assess student learning.
c. improve instruction.
d. assess student learning and improve instruction.

Question 3 Testing and reteaching should be viewed as

a. an integral and normal part of instruction.
b. a sign of an incompetent instructor.
c. punishment for poor work habits.
d. a rarely used activity.

Question 4 The term *instructional alignment* refers to the relationship

a. among the classroom furniture.
b. among curriculum, instruction, and testing.
c. between instruction and testing.
d. between curriculum and testing.

Question 5 The student error rate in guided practice

a. determines student grades.
b. determines when independent practice can be initiated.
c. should be at least 50 percent.
d. should be at least 75 percent.

Question 6 Teacher "withitness" is related to

a. monitoring and moving around the entire class.
b. a relevant curriculum.

c. an appreciation of teenage cultural trends.

d. identifying with faddish instruction.

Question 7 Effective teaching is characterized by

a. student compliance with authority.

b. extensive student choices.

c. student-directed instruction and a range of alternate activities.

d. productive student engagement and careful teacher supervision.

Question 8 The goals and the quality of assignments should be

a. clarified by the teacher.

b. clarified by the student.

c. unimportant for good students.

d. left unclear to add a challenge.

Question 9 If a course is taught once a day, the daily testing should be supplemented with at least

a. a monthly comprehensive diagnostic mastery test.

b. an end-of-course test.

c. a weekly comprehensive diagnostic mastery test.

d. an annual standardized test.

Question 10 Student performance on prerequisite skills determines

a. what grade the student receives.

b. how difficult the lesson will be.

c. the students who will succeed.

d. whether the new content will be introduced immediately.

Fill in the Blanks

Question 11 Monitoring should emphasize the _____ of instruction rather than the classification of teaching practices.

Question 12 Monitoring should emphasize _____, not just the storage of data.

Question 13 Mastery testing should emphasize success levels of _____ or better.

Question 14 Research has turned up _____ _____ evidence suggesting the need for qualitatively different levels of instruction for students who differ in aptitude, achievement level, socioeconomic status, ethnicity, or learning style.

Question 15 The effectiveness of mastery-based testing is increased when the _____ is increased.

Answer Key: Knowledge Quiz (Academic Monitoring)

Multiple Choice

Question 1 The term *instructionally diagnostic* refers to

c. the cross-referencing between test items and instructional elements.

Question 2 Monitoring is conducted to

d. assess student learning and improve instruction.

Question 3 Testing and reteaching should be viewed as

a. an integral and normal part of instruction.

Question 4 The term *instructional alignment* refers to the relationship

b. among curriculum, instruction, and testing.

Question 5 The student error rate in guided practice

b. determines when independent practice can be initiated.

Question 6 Teacher "withitness" is related to

a. monitoring and moving around the entire class.

Question 7 Effective teaching is characterized by

d. productive student engagement and careful teacher supervision.

Question 8 The goals and the quality of assignments should be

a. clarified by the teacher.

Question 9 If a course is taught once a day, the daily testing should be supplemented with at least

c. a weekly comprehensive diagnostic mastery test.

Question 10 Student performance on prerequisite skills determines

d. whether the new content will be introduced immediately.

Fill in the Blanks

Question 11   Monitoring should emphasize the *improvement* of instruction rather than the classification of teaching practices.

Question 12   Monitoring should emphasize *decision-making*, not just the storage of data.

Question 13   Mastery testing should emphasize success levels of *90 percent* or better.

Question 14   Research has turned up *very little* evidence suggesting the need for qualitatively different levels of instruction for students who differ in aptitude, achievement level, socioeconomic status, ethnicity, or learning style.

Question 15   The effectiveness of mastery-based testing is increased when the *feedback* is increased.

C. Self-evaluation Checklist: Academic Monitoring

Instructions for Completing the Self-evaluation Checklist

The self-evaluation checklist on the following pages should be completed using the following scale and criteria.

1 = No change is needed in present practices.
2 = There are minor problems that can be corrected quickly and easily.
3 = There are major problems that will require a considerable investment in time and effort.
4 = I need more specific information on my own behavior before I can decide whether I have a problem.

The evaluation questions are provided as a guide to the type of specific behaviors that exemplify each of the effective teaching skills. You should feel free to add evaluation questions if you feel that they will increase the practicality and sensitivity of the evaluation process.

Please make supporting notes that will help describe any problems in more detail. Notes should address the context; for example, certain problems may be more or less noticeable, depending on the time, the class, the individual student, the lesson activity, and the subject being taught.

If the space provided on the evaluation checklist is not sufficient, supplement the checklist by adding descriptive material and cross-referencing supplementary material with the number of the skill and the letter of the evaluation question (e.g., Skill 2, Question c).

Additional information on the criteria and the use of the self-evaluation checklist is provided in Section C of Chapter 2.

Self-evaluation Checklist

Skill 1. Assignment Clarification
Students understand what is expected of them.

Evaluation Questions	Rating and Notes	
a. Are students required to demonstrate that they know how to accomplish assignments?		
b. Are students taught how to use self-monitoring procedures to evaluate their assignments?		
c. Are assignments written out rather than presented orally?		
d. Is there a clear procedure for communicating with parents regarding homework assignments?		

Skill 2. Assignment Follow-up
Students are expected to complete their work according to established standards and deadlines.

Evaluation Questions	Rating and Notes	
a. Are the format requirements of assignments in terms of length, neatness, and accuracy specified?		
b. Are students required to make corrections to inaccurate or incomplete assignments?		
c. Does the grading of assignments reward accurate and timely completion?		
d. Do assignment correction procedures diagnose subskill deficits?		

Rating Scale: 1 - No change; 2 - Minor problems; 3 - Major problems; 4 - Insufficient information

Skill 3. Seatwork Monitoring
During seatwork, the teacher circulates around the classroom, checking all students' work and providing assistance to students.

Evaluation Questions	Rating and Notes	
a. Does the physical layout of the room facilitate easy movement among students' desks?		
b. Are random selections of students' work checked during independent seatwork?		
c. Are students encouraged to recognize when they need help and ask for it?		

Skill 4. Daily Monitoring
Students' work products are monitored on a daily basis and rates of learning and levels of understanding or performance monitored.

Evaluation Questions	Rating and Notes	
a. Are cues from students used to modify instruction during a presentation?		
b. Are students required to demonstrate understanding during instructional presentations?		
c. Does teacher recordkeeping monitor individual skill acquisition?		
d. Are worksheets checked in an accurate and timely fashion?		

Skill 5. Instructional Alignment
Academic monitoring reflects alignment among curriculum, instruction, and testing.

Evaluation Questions	Rating and Notes	
a. Do comprehensive tests of student mastery adequately sample the instructional content?		
b. Do comprehensive tests of student mastery adequately sample the required curriculum?		
c. Are test results used to adjust instructional procedures for the class as a whole?		
d. Are test results used to adjust instructional procedures for individuals?		
e. Does the instruction focus on the curriculum?		

D. Information Gathering: Academic Monitoring

This section includes two forms that may be used to gather information on monitoring your classroom: Form 5.1, "Academic Monitoring," can be used to monitor homework assignments, and Form 5.2, "Interaction Monitoring," will help monitor verbal interactions with students. Directions for using the forms are included.

The Academic Monitoring Form

Form 5.1 can be used to monitor the performance of your students on independent work (homework). The form provides a format for making decisions about students who need to make corrections and those who need reteaching. (See the partially completed sample, Form 5.1a.)

The first step in using Form 5.1b is to specify the criteria to be met for "passing off" the assignment without corrections, making corrections, and receiving reteaching. Please refer to the completed sample (Form 5.1a) if you have questions regarding how to use the monitoring form.

Academic Monitoring

Subject _Math_

Names	Date 3/23 Prepared	Criteria → Scores ↓	85-95%	Below 85%	C	R	Date 3/24 Prepared	Criteria → Scores ↓	C	R	Date 3/25 Prepared	Criteria → Scores ↓	C	R	Date 3/26 Prepared	Criteria → Scores ↓	C	R	Date 3/27 Prepared	Criteria → Scores ↓	C	R
Bob H.	N																					
Kris H.	N	75				R																
David H.	Y	100																				
Maryanne P.	Y	87			¢																	
Yim L.	Y	97																				
Todd S.	Y	98																				
Mark T.	N	60				R																
Terry M.	Y	70				R																
Bill L.	Y	90			C																	
Penny H.	Y	87			C																	
Gail D.	Y	96																				
Lonnie T.	Y	99																				
Mark H.	Y	86			¢																	
Mike R.	N	63				R																

* **Prepared:** Students have homework finished on time. (Y=Yes, N=No)

Criteria: Specify the criteria for C= Correcting Work and R= Reteaching work with teacher before correcting. When recording scores, record a "C" or "R" if students need to correct homework or be retaught. When work has been corrected or retaught put a slash through the "C" or "R."

Academic Monitoring

Subject _____

Names	Prepared	Criteria → Scores ↓	C	R	Prepared	Criteria → Scores ↓	C	R	Prepared	Criteria → Scores ↓	C	R	Prepared	Criteria → Scores ↓	C	R	Prepared	Criteria → Scores ↓	C	R

Date_____   Date_____   Date_____   Date_____   Date_____

* Prepared: Students have homework finished on time. (Y=Yes, N=No)

Criteria: Specify the criteria for C= Correcting Work and R= Reteaching work with teacher before correcting. When recording scores, record a "C" or "R" if students need to correct homework or be retaught. When work has been corrected or retaught put a slash through the "C" or "R."

Interaction Monitoring

Form 5.2 is designed to help you monitor the verbal interactions between teachers and students. The form has three major categories to be filled in: Initiator, Type of Interaction, and Quality of Interaction. In addition, columns for students' names and comments are included. To use the form, please tape-record or videotape a class session, and then analyze each of the verbal interactions in terms of the three major categories. (See the partially completed sample, Form 5.2a.)

The initiator of the interaction is the source of the interaction: either the teacher or the student.

The type of interaction may be procedural, behavioral, or academic. Procedural interactions are requests that have to do with housekeeping chores, seeking permission, and reporting nonacademic assignments. Behavioral interactions are comments that deal with classroom behavior such as verbal participation, talk, and student movement in the classroom. An academic interaction is one that is work-related, including contacts that have to do with the instructional presentations and students' completion of seatwork, homework, or other academic assignments.

In the Quality of Interaction column, fill in a judgment about the nature of the interaction. A positive interaction is one that is posed in a positive, accepting manner. The interaction may involve praise. A neutral interaction is one that is posed in a matter-of-fact manner. A negative interaction is one that is posed in a negative, critical manner.

Class *Math*	Date *2/19/88*	Page *1* of *4*
Event *Fractions Review*	Time: Start *9:08* Stop *9:50*	Elapsed *42 min.*

Initiator	Type of Interaction	Student's Name/Group	Quality of Interaction	Comments:
S Ⓣ	Ⓟ B A	*Group*	+ ⊙ -	*Take out your books.*
S Ⓣ	Ⓟ B A	*"*	+ ⊙ -	*I hope everyone has*
S T	P B A		+ o -	*their work finished.*
Ⓢ T	Ⓟ B A	*Tom*	+ ⊙ -	*Can I sharpen my*
S T	P B A		+ o -	*pencil?*
S Ⓣ	P B Ⓐ	*Group*	+ ⊙ -	*Today we will ...*
S Ⓣ	P B Ⓐ	*Jim*	⊕ o -	*Good! Tell us about...*
S T	P B A		+ o -	
S T	P B A		+ o -	
S T	P B A		+ o -	
S T	P B A		+ o -	
S T	P B A		+ o -	
S T	P B A		+ o -	
S T	P B A		+ o -	
S T	P B A		+ o -	
S T	P B A		+ o -	
S T	P B A		+ o -	
S T	P B A		+ o -	
S T	P B A		+ o -	
S T	P B A		+ o -	
S T	P B A		+ o -	
S T	P B A		+ o -	
S T	P B A		+ o -	
S T	P B A		+ o -	
S T	P B A		+ o -	

S = Student, T= Teacher; P= Procedural, B= Behavioral, A= Academic; + = Positive, o = Neutral, - = Negative

| Class _____ | Date _____ | Page ____ of ____ |
| Event _____ | Time: Start _____ Stop _____ Elapsed _____ | |

Initiator	Type of Interaction	Student's Name/Group	Quality of Interaction	Comments:
S T	P B A		+ o -	
S T	P B A		+ o -	
S T	P B A		+ o -	
S T	P B A		+ o -	
S T	P B A		+ o -	
S T	P B A		+ o -	
S T	P B A		+ o -	
S T	P B A		+ o -	
S T	P B A		+ o -	
S T	P B A		+ o -	
S T	P B A		+ o -	
S T	P B A		+ o -	
S T	P B A		+ o -	
S T	P B A		+ o -	
S T	P B A		+ o -	
S T	P B A		+ o -	
S T	P B A		+ o -	
S T	P B A		+ o -	
S T	P B A		+ o -	
S T	P B A		+ o -	
S T	P B A		+ o -	
S T	P B A		+ o -	
S T	P B A		+ o -	
S T	P B A		+ o -	
S T	P B A		+ o -	
S T	P B A		+ o -	
S T	P B A		+ o -	

S = Student, T= Teacher; P= Procedural, B= Behavioral, A= Academic; + = Positive, o = Neutral, - = Negative

E. Practical Suggestions: Academic Monitoring

The practical suggestions in this section represent a collection of ideas based on classroom observations, experience, and a reviewing of the effective teaching literature and teacher magazines. Feel free to incorporate any of the suggestions that work for you.

Monitoring and Goals

a. Set Reasonable Standards.

(1) Specify the format requirements of the assignments in terms of length, neatness, accuracy, and type of materials to be used.

(2) Give students a general idea of how much time an assignment should take to complete.

(3) If homework is appropriately assigned in terms of difficulty level, you should be able to require a high level of accuracy.

(4) Provide models of what you would like written products to look like.

(5) Inform your students of your expectations for completing homework.

(6) When work is incomplete, require that students redo assignments until the work meets expectations.

b. Maintain Due Dates.

(1) Extend deadlines and relax standards only rarely. Do so for the entire class, not just for individual students.

(2) Ask students often about their work plans and their progress.

(3) Frequently communicate an interest in the topic that students are working on.

(4) Help students by reminding them of their assignments and the amount of time they have remaining to complete the assignments.

(5) Show students how to keep track of their assignments by making lists and crossing off assignments as they are completed. You can begin to teach this self-monitoring procedure by giving students a list of the classes for a given day and having them cross off the class when it is over.

(6) Establish consequences for failing to complete homework. Set up a separate area in the classroom where students who have not completed their assignments can work while you are correcting homework. Keep extra copies of assignments and books for students who leave their work at home.

Providing for Timely Monitoring

    a. Circulate around the Classroom.

        (1) First, make certain that the work has been well chosen and explained so that most students will be progressing smoothly through the assignment rather than waiting for help.

        (2) Most of your interactions with students should be fairly brief.

        (3) Make certain the physical layout of your classroom facilitates movement among students' desks.

        (4) Have a few extra chairs available so that you can easily sit down while helping a student.

        (5) Don't plan to get involved with any other project, such as correcting papers, when you need to be circulating among students.

        (6) Ask students to try working on another portion of the assignment while they are waiting for your assistance.

    b. Help All Students.

        (1) Monitor the work of all students, not just those who ask for help.

        (2) Try to get students to recognize when they need help and ask for it.

        (3) Randomly check parts of students' work when you are circulating. For example, if a student is working on a math worksheet, randomly select a problem and correct it.

        (4) If students are having difficulty staying on-task, or if you want to monitor them closely, draw a line on their worksheets and tell them to raise their hands when they get to that point.

        (5) Divide your time and attention among all students.

        (6) Ask students to show you their work.

Decision Making and Corrective Action

    a. Give Clear Directions.

        (1) Keep assignments varied and interesting.

        (2) Go over practice examples with students.

        (3) Have students demonstrate that they know how to accomplish the requirements in the assignment.

        (4) Keep homework assignments for elementary-aged students fairly brief (10–15 minutes per evening). Many school districts have established homework time recommendations for each grade level. Check your district's policy.

(5) Try to provide students with positive learning experiences that integrate material presented in class and thus help students develop more appropriate attitudes about school and their ability to learn.

(6) Don't give directions for two or more new activities within the same time period.

(7) Help students remember assignments by writing them on the chalkboard rather than presenting them orally.

(8) Make certain students know what work they are accountable for, how to get help if they need it, and what to do when they finish.

(9) Make certain students keep assignments in a special notebook or on a specially printed form.

b. Monitor Understanding.

(1) Monitor students' scores. Use monitoring information to make decisions regarding future assignments.

(2) Provide feedback and follow-up. Reteach and correct errors when necessary.

(3) Make certain students are experiencing high success levels (90 to 100 percent) on homework assignments.

(4) Monitor student progress in terms of completion and accuracy.

(5) Elicit the cooperation of parents in encouraging students to be responsible for completing homework assignments.

Monitoring and the Improvement of Instruction

a. Check Students' Progress during Instruction.

(1) Validate and modify instruction on the basis of cues that surface during the lesson. For example, if students seem confused, stop and find out why before continuing with your presentation.

(2) Have students give choral responses during instruction. If the choral response is weak, it is possible that students are confused.

(3) Ask students for a show of hands in response to a question regarding the content of the information you are presenting.

(4) Ask students to make a brief written response that you can inspect quickly.

(5) When you are checking a particular answer on a worksheet, ask students to point to the answer with their pencil so that you can find the problem quickly.

(6) When students have finished working a problem, ask them to lay their pencils on top of their papers.

b. Check Students' Progress after Instruction.

    (1) Build time into your schedule to correct papers on a daily basis.

    (2) Use answer keys to facilitate quick checking of worksheets. Even if it only saves you a few seconds per worksheet, you'll be surprised how much time it saves you on a set of worksheets.

    (3) Use monitoring forms to facilitate record-keeping procedures. Use separate forms for each content area. The monitoring forms can be set up for individual students or for a group of students. Keep these forms in an accessible location in file folders or on clipboards, and fill them out daily.

    (4) If you use traditional gradebooks, use different-colored ink pens to record grades. By doing so, you can quickly see how well the group or an individual student is doing.

F. Self-improvement Plan: Academic Monitoring

After completing the self-evaluation checklist (Section C) and reading through the practical suggestions (Section E), you should be prepared to develop a self-improvement plan (SIP). Please complete portion A, entitled "Academic Monitoring: Goals and Objectives," on the self-improvement plan by checking the goal(s) and objective(s) you wish to include in your plan. Also, write a brief narrative describing how you plan to address the requirements in portions B–E. Complete portion F, "Results," after you have completed your self-improvement implementation project. (See Chapter 2, Section F, for a completed self-improvement plan.)

Self-improvement Plan: Academic Monitoring

Name _____ Class _____ Date _____

A. Academic Monitoring: Goals and Objectives
   1. Monitoring and Goals
      a. Set reasonable standards.
      b. Maintain due dates.
      c. Other _____
   2. Providing for Timely Monitoring
      a. Circulate around the classroom.
      b. Help all students.
      c. Other _____
   3. Decision Making and Corrective Action
      a. Give clear directions.
      b. Monitor understanding.
      c. Other _____
   4. Monitoring and the Improvement of Instruction
      a. Check students' progress during instruction.
      b. Check students' progress after instruction.
      c. Other _____

B. Practical Suggestions
Please indicate which of the practical suggestions from Section E you plan to use to meet each of the objectives. (You may include practical suggestions from other sources as well.)

C. Specific Procedures
Please describe the specific procedures you will use to implement the practical suggestions.

D. Current and Desired Performance
Please describe your current performance and desired performance in regard to each of the objectives you have selected. You may state the performance in terms of student behavior, such as percentage of due dates met.

E. Timelines and Change Measures
Please describe your timelines and how you will measure change in relationship to the objectives you have selected.

F. Results
Upon completion of your self-improvement project, please submit copies of this form and a brief description of the result of its implementation. Attach any raw data sheets that were used to gather information and describe any changes that were made during your project.

References

Bickel, W.E., & Bickel, D.D. (1986). Effective schools, classrooms, and instruction: Implications for special education. *Exceptional Children, 52*, 489–500.

Bloom, B.S. (1968, May). Mastery learning. *Evaluation Comment, 1*(2). Los Angeles: University of California at Los Angeles, Center for the Study of Evaluation of Instructional Programs.

Brophy, J. (1987). *Research linking teacher behavior to student achievement: Potential implications for instruction of Chapter I students.* Unpublished manuscript, Michigan State University, East Lansing, Mich.

Brophy, J., & Good, T. (1986). Teacher behavior and student achievement. In M.C. Wittrock (Ed.), *Handbook of research on teaching,* 3rd ed. (pp. 328–375). New York: Macmillan.

Cohen, A. (1987). Instructional alignment: Searching for a magic bullet. *Educational Researcher, 16*(8), 16–20.

Fisher, C.W., Berliner, D.C., Filby, N.N., Marliave, R., Cahen, L.S., & Dishaw, M.M. (1980). Teaching behaviors, academic learning time and student achievement: An overview. In C. Denham & A. Lieberman (Eds.), *Time to learn* (pp. 7–32). Washington, D.C.: U.S. Department of Education, National Institute of Education.

Good, T.L., Grouws, D.A., & Ebmeier, H. (1983). *Active mathematics teaching.* New York: Longman.

Hahn, A. (1987). Reaching to America's dropouts: What to do? *Phi Delta Kappan, 69*(4), 256–263.

Kulik, C.C., & Kulik, J.A. (1987). Mastery testing and student learning: A meta-analysis. *Journal of Educational Technology Systems, 15*(3), 325–345.

Rosenshine, B. (1979). Content, time, and direction instruction. In P. Peterson & H. Walberg (Eds.), *Research on teaching: Concepts, findings, and implications.* Berkeley, Calif.: McCutchan.

Rosenshine, B., & Stevens, R. (1986). Teaching functions. In M.C. Wittrock (Ed.), *Handbook of research on teaching,* 3rd ed. (pp. 376–391). New York: Macmillan.

CHAPTER 6

Classroom Management

A. The Research Literature
   Management and Order
   Classroom Management Concepts
   Summary: Effective Classroom Management and the
      Profession
B. Knowledge Quiz: Classroom Management
   Answer Key: Knowledge Quiz (Classroom
      Management)
C. Self-evaluation Checklist: Classroom Management
   Instructions for Completing the Self-evaluation
      Checklist
   Self-evaluation Checklist
D. Information Gathering: Classroom Management
   School Rules
   Daily Goals
E. Practical Suggestions: Classroom Management
   Setting and Implementing Rules
   Managing Interventions
   Increasing Appropriate Behavior
F. Self-improvement Plan: Classroom Management
References

A. The Research Literature

Management and Order

Classroom management has been defined as the provisions and procedures necessary to establish and maintain an environment in which instruction and learning can occur (Duke, 1979). The primary goal of effective classroom management is not the reduction of misbehavior or even the creation of an "orderly" environment (see Figure 6.1). Although they are related issues, effective classroom management and the establishment of order are not synonymous. For example, teaching practices that lead to passive nonengagement would not threaten an orderly environment, but would reduce opportunities for learning (Doyle, 1986). Student learning is the primary goal of effective classroom management.

Although the presence of order in a classroom does not necessarily indicate high levels of learning, the research clearly suggests that an emphasis on effective strategies to promote learning can facilitate order. Doyle (1984) reported that effective teachers in difficult management situations pushed students through the curriculum as a way of achieving and sustaining order.

Classroom Management Concepts

Instructional Strength. In summarizing the findings from the research, Doyle (1986) made the observation that the quality of classroom management depends on "the strength and durability of the primary program, or vector of action" (p. 393). In essence, then, the essential prerequisite for effective classroom management is *instructional strength* in the implementation of:

1. Time management procedures, such as appropriate pacing and well-planned transitions
2. Teaching functions, such as attention to prerequisites, guided practice and systematic reviews
3. Effective academic feedback and monitoring skills

Instructional strength supports a teacher's efforts to bring about both learning and order in a classroom.

Although it seems obvious to state that effective classroom management is facilitated if students are actively and successfully engaged in the planned program of instruction, most teachers know that it is easy to be distracted by student misbehavior and therefore to forget to stress the primary instructional tasks. A vicious cycle can be created, in which lack of attention to the

FIGURE 6.1

The Emphasis in Classroom Management

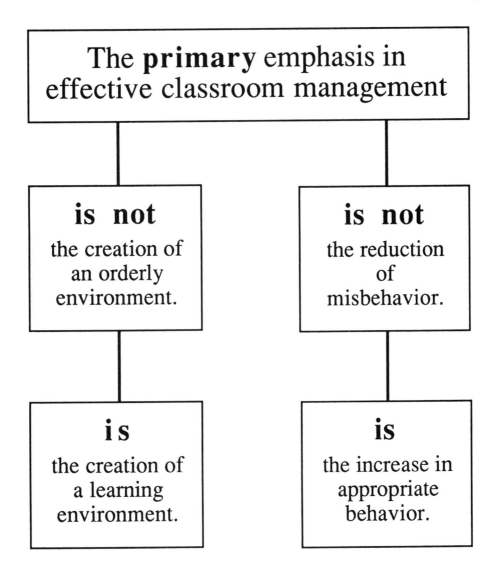

primary instructional tasks creates the vacuum in which misbehavior thrives, and this misbehavior further distracts the teacher from the primary instructional tasks.

The effective teacher knows full well that effective class management is not primarily the process of reducing misbehavior, but rather the process of increasing appropriate behavior.

Setting and Implementing Rules.   In summarizing the findings from a study that involved the intense observation of classroom management procedures in 75 elementary school classrooms, Crocker and Brooker (1986) stated that "higher achievement is attained in classrooms that function in a businesslike manner, under high teacher direction, with a minimum of lost time or task disruption" (p. 10).

Teachers who operate classrooms in a businesslike manner explicitly communicate not only the goals of the instruction but also the rules students need to follow, so as to ensure a productive interaction between teaching procedures and student behavior. To the casual observer, the process of rule setting appears to inform students of new expectations. The effective classroom manager realizes that the process of rule setting is far more complex and subtle. In reality, most students in most grades already know the rules. What, then, is the primary purpose of rule setting if it is not the imparting of new information? The issue has been summarized by Doyle (1986) as follows:

> By setting rules, a teacher communicates his or her awareness of what can happen in a classroom and demonstrates a degree of commitment to work. Students are thus able to acquire valuable information early in the year about a teacher's approach and expectations for behavior. The more explicit the rules and the more clearly they are communicated, the more likely the teacher will care about maintaining order and not tolerate inappropriate and disruptive behavior. But simply stating the rules is not enough. A teacher must also demonstrate a willingness and an ability to act when rules are broken [p. 413].

Rules should have a strong preventive role. For example, if a teacher constantly reprimands students for playing with objects on their desks and sets no rules related to what should be on the desk for a specific activity, he or she has failed to make use of a simple preventive option—the use of a set of rules to guide the effective use of desk space in school and in future work places.

The process of setting and implementing rules has instructional as well as management value. The students are learning procedures for ensuring their effective participation and acceptance in social settings. For this reason, rules should be introduced in the same way as any academic concept is introduced. The rationale for the rules should be clarified, and the processes used to present the rules should promote both understanding and respect for the rules. Rules should not be defined and followed just "because the teacher says so."

Managing Interventions. The process of monitoring student behavior and intervening when necessary is clearly one of the most demanding requirements for effective classroom management. The need for interventions is reduced if credible rules are clarified and instructional activities are appropriately implemented, but there may still be several times in each lesson when some type of intervention is necessary.

The misbehavior being addressed in this discussion is the kind teachers typically encounter. Typical misbehaviors include tardiness, cutting classes, failure to bring supplies and books, inattentiveness, talking, call-outs, and mild forms of verbal and physical aggression (Silverstein, 1979).

The propensity for student misbehavior is clearly related to students' perceptions of the teacher as a manager. One way the teacher establishes credibility is by demonstrating an awareness of who will probably misbehave, and when. The research has consistently documented the fact that most misbehavior is initiated by only a few students (Metz, 1978). We also know that the time and the type of task are factors in predicting the occurrence of misbehavior. Rusnock and Brandler (1979) noted that higher-ability students were more prone to misbehavior during transitions and near the end of instructional segments. Lower-ability students were more likely to be off-task in the middle of an instructional segment.

The teacher who demonstrates an awareness of times of high probability for misbehavior, and exercises increased vigilance or takes other preventive action, is building credibility and preventing the occurrence of misbehavior. The teacher who, for example, initiates a transition and then turns to write on the blackboard is inviting challenges and reducing credibility.

The teacher's physical placement in the classroom can create or reduce opportunities for monitoring student behavior and managing interventions. The teacher who spends virtually all class time at the front of the class will not have the opportunity to observe what is really going on at each desk, nor will he or she be able to make the timely and personal contacts that build productive relationships between teacher and students. The effective teacher is very aware that management is far easier from the back than from the front of the classroom.

There is little in the research literature to suggest that there is a positive correlation between the frequency of interventions to reduce misbehavior and student achievement. Kounin (1983), in an observational study, noted that the least successful teacher in the study conducted 986 interventions to reduce misbehavior in one day. During that same day, the students were "on-task" in the same classroom only 25 percent of the time.

Interventions range from relatively unobtrusive signals to extremely disruptive actions. The less obtrusive signals would include such actions as pointing to the student's notepad, eye contact, proximity, and gesturing by touching a finger to the lips or ear to prompt the student to stop talking or to listen. Teacher statements such as "Wait," "My turn," "Jane's turn," and "Stop" can be very effective if the statements are delivered quickly and serve to terminate an inappropriate utterance or action without interrupting the lesson activity.

Interventions that interrupt the flow of the lesson and invite negotiation or discussion at an inappropriate time can be counterproductive. Teacher statements such as "Weren't you here when we discussed the rules on talking during seatwork?" open up class time to unnecessary and inappropriate discussions. Rules have little value if the teacher is not absolutely certain that all students know and understand them.

One intervention that preserves the flow of the lesson is the use of a work assignment to terminate an inappropriate behavior. Having the student answer a question does a number of things. It keeps the class focused on the learning task, serves notice to the student that the teacher is monitoring the student's behavior, and assigns the student a task that is usually incompatible with the inappropriate behavior.

If an intervention can't be handled quickly, the teacher should not interrupt the flow of the instruction, but rather set the class a task that ensures its active engagement while freeing the teacher to deal with the problem and with the student or students involved. One clear advantage to taking time to make sure the class is productively engaged is that it reduces the possibility of an irrational, negative response by the teacher. If the teacher takes a little time to "cool down" and plan the interaction, an unproductive confrontation can be avoided. The teacher can then use the opportunity to model appropriate social processes, such as asking the students to explain their perceptions of the problem before sharing the reasons for the teacher's concern.

More extreme forms of intervention, such as parental contacts and sending students to the principal's office, may be necessary, but they should be viewed as a sign of a breakdown in classroom management. The effective classroom manager will conduct a "post-mortem" each time a more extreme intervention has been used, to see whether other management procedures might be more effective. The excessive use of mild interventions should also prompt a review of instructional practices.

One form of intervention is *task engagement feedback:* feedback to the student about whether classroom behavior is acceptable or unacceptable. After intensely observing a large number of teachers, a group of researchers (Fisher et al., 1980) reported as follows:

> Most of the task engagement feedback we observed turned out to be negative, such as reminders to students to get back to work when they were off task. We found no evidence that frequent use of such reprimands had any positive effect. It may be that some well-timed and well-phrased reminders are useful, but when task engagement feedback becomes frequent, it is a sign that some structural changes are needed. There is an important lesson here for teachers who use these findings to increase student engagement: Scolding students more often is not the answer. Instead, one might (1) check to see that tasks are not too hard for the student (task engagement feedback was positively correlated with low success rate), (2) increase the clarity and emphasis with which expectations are stated and the consistency with which students are held accountable, or (3) increase the amount of substantive interactive instruction [p. 28].

Increasing Appropriate Behavior.   Clearly, one of the most important types of appropriate behavior is success in the curriculum, and such success must be followed by timely reinforcing consequences. However, other competencies are often required of students, and these are not always formally stated. Trenholm and Rose (1981) identified the following categories: responding in appropriate form to academic requests or tasks, controlling impulsiveness, dealing with problems and negative feedback in mature ways, interacting courteously and cooperatively with peers, attending to and becoming involved in classroom activities and procedures, and recognizing appropriate contexts for different types of behavior. If the teacher feels that any of these behaviors are important, he or she should say so and possibly post a list of them. It is unfair and instructionally ineffective to expect a student to deduce a teacher's "silent curriculum" by observing or experiencing the teacher's system of rewards and punishments.

The *silent* (or *hidden*) *curriculum* refers to the nonacademic curriculum modeled and implied in the management procedures used by the teacher. Affective goals such as "respect for others," "improved self-concept," and "increased desire for learning" are modeled by the instructional and management practices in use in the classroom.

Perhaps the most frequently mentioned consequence for appropriate behavior is teacher praise. Researchers who have observed the use of praise in the classroom suggest that all is not well. Brophy (1981), in a summary of the research, reported that "Classroom-process data indicate teachers' verbal praise cannot be equated with reinforcement. Typically, such praise is used infrequently, without contingency, specificity, or credibility" (p. 5).

In an effort to exemplify effective and ineffective procedures for using praise in the classroom, Brophy (1981) provided a listing of examples. Table 6.1 is an adaption of the original listing.

Reducing Reprimands and Punishments.   One of the most unfortunate misconceptions that can develop in a classroom is the confusion of academic errors with misbehavior. Students should be required to do their best, but they cannot be required to be successful on every response. If an affective climate is created in which students feel punished for making errors, whether subtly or overtly, then errors will have been equated with misbehavior. Such confusion can easily occur and must be guarded against.

The psychological climate created by the teacher's feedback procedures should be a critical element in keeping errors from being equated with misbehavior. If a reprimand is associated with an error, it must be made clear that the teacher's concern addresses the perceived cause of the error (e.g., homework not done) rather than the error itself. If the teacher uses reprimands, the same rules that are suggested for delivering praise must be followed. The reprimands should be contingent, specific, and credible.

If reprimands are too general and given too often, the long-term consequences can be devastating for student and teacher. Common consequences include confusion of errors with punishment;

TABLE 6.1 Guidelines for Effective Praise

Effective Praise	Ineffective Praise
1. Is delivered contingently (e.g., it is clearly linked in time with the student action)	1. Is delivered randomly or unsystematically
2. Specifies the particulars of the accomplishment (e.g., "good, you recognized the incomplete sentence")	2. Is restricted to global positive reactions (e.g., "good")
3. Shows spontaneity, variety, and other signs of credibility; suggests clear attention to student's accomplishment	3. Shows a bland uniformity, which suggests a conditioned response made with minimal attention
4. Rewards attainment of specified performance criteria (which can include effort criteria, however)	4. Rewards mere participation, without consideration of performance processes or outcomes
5. Provides information to students about their competence or the value of their accomplishments	5. Provides no information at all or gives students information about their status
6. Orients students toward better appreciation of their own task-related behavior and thinking about problem solving	6. Orients students toward comparing themselves with others and competing (e.g., "well, at least you did better than Jean")
7. Uses students' own prior accomplishments as the context for describing present accomplishments	7. Uses the accomplishments of peers as the context for describing students' present accomplishments
8. Is given in recognition of noteworthy effort or success at difficult (for this student) tasks (e.g., "you hung in there and made it!")	8. Is given without regard to the effort expended or the meaning of the accomplishment (for this student)
9. Attributes success to effort and ability, implying that similar successes can be expected in the future	9. Attributes success to ability alone or to external factors such as luck or easy task (e.g., "lucky guess")
10. Fosters endogenous attributions (students believe that they expend effort on the task because they enjoy the task and/or want to develop task-relevant skills)	10. Fosters exogenous attributions (students believe that they expend effort on the task for external reasons--to please the teacher, win a competition or reward, etc.)
11. Focuses students' attention on their own task-relevant behavior (e.g., "well done, you have really practiced reading")	11. Focuses students' attention on the teacher as an external authority figure who is manipulating them
12. Fosters appreciation of and desirable attributions about task-relevant behavior after the process is completed	12. Intrudes into the ongoing process, distracting attention from task-relevant behavior

a lowered student self-concept, which further decreases the student's interest in the curriculum; and reduced effect of the reprimand, which causes the students to take less notice of teacher statements. The following guidelines are suggested for verbal reprimands:

1. If reprimands are used, make sure that they are used sparingly and effectively.
2. Make certain that praise statements greatly outnumber verbal reprimands.
3. Ensure that no student is consistently subjected to verbal reprimands. The impact of a reprimand will vary with the student and the content, but if any student consistently receives more than one reprimand for every ten positive or neutral statements, the teachers should search for alternate instructional procedures.

In the short term, verbal reprimands and other punishment delivered in a public and personally destructive manner can be very effective in stopping a specific misbehavior. For this reason, a teacher can be trapped into increasing such responses to student misbehavior. Again, the long-term consequences of such teacher actions can be devastating for teacher and student. The teacher loses the respect of all students, and reprimands lose their effectiveness—future reprimands have to be even more personally destructive to be effective. The cycle of a gradually increasing emphasis on reprimands and decreasing student sensitivity to reprimands has been documented by a number of researchers. Becker (1986) refers to it as the "the criticism trap" (see Figure 6.2).

If a public reprimand is called for, the following suggestions are offered to minimize the damage and increase the effectiveness of the action.

1. Address the specific action, not the person, as undesirable.
2. Give a reason why the behavior is undesirable.
3. Provide a suggestion for a more appropriate behavior to address the underlying concern of the student and to replace the undesirable behavior with an incompatible, appropriate behavior.
4. Very often the underlying concern is valid, even though the form of expression is inappropriate. Validate the concern, not the inappropriate expression: "You have every right to be bored while waiting for me to check your paper, and I will get to you quickly next time. However, writing your initials on the desk is destroying a community resource. Erase it and start working on the next assignment while you are waiting."
5. Take every opportunity to praise the individual for appropriate behavior during the remainder of the class.
6. Never imply by word or action that you are expressing a personal dislike for the student.

FIGURE 6.2

Reprimands— A Trap for the Unwary

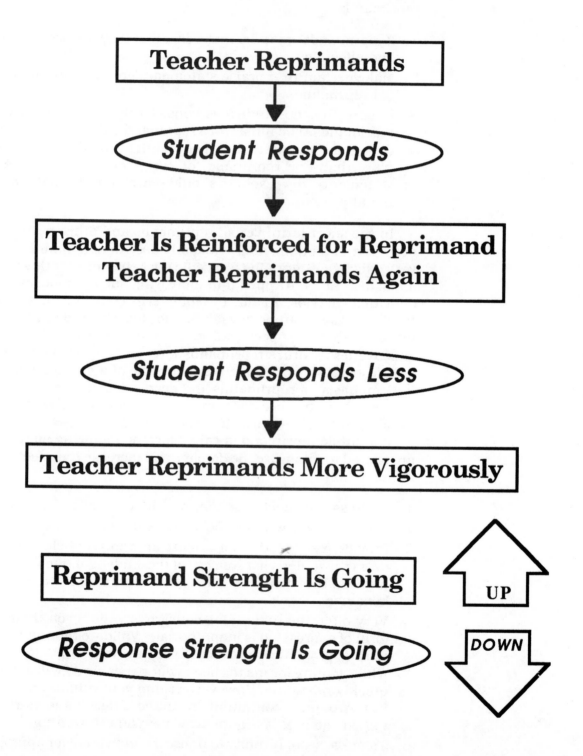

One problem with punishment arises from the uncertainty of the consequences. Even a mild reprimand can be psychologically devastating for some very sensitive students but absolutely meaningless to other students. For some students, including those with chronic misbehavior, negative teacher attention can actually increase the misbehavior. One research summary reported that "any teacher attention (including reprimand) to the misbehavior of students with behavior problems may increase the frequency of the misbehavior" (Morsink, Soar, Soar, & Thomas, 1986, p. 35).

A teacher obviously cannot ignore all student misbehavior, since some misbehavior involves psychological and physical risk to the student and others, but any decision to give negative attention to students must be weighed carefully. The problems associated with punishment only increase the importance of prevention and early intervention before problems become severe.

Summary: Effective Classroom Management and the Profession

Most experienced teachers have encountered a few peers trapped in a vicious cycle in which they are heavily dependent on reprimands and punishment as the primary vehicles for attempting to create order and reduce misbehavior. Such an approach to management strips teacher and students of dignity and threatens the credibility and professionalism of all teachers.

In contrast, teachers who clarify the "hidden curriculum" effectively implement a well-planned and validated sequence of instruction, and frequently recognize and praise students thereby add to the credibility of the profession and have more positive feelings about themselves as persons and as educators. It has been reported that although effective teachers work hard, they rarely have difficulty "coping." Hosford (1984) summed up the issue as follows:

> Effective teachers manage well. Coping is rarely an issue. The students are so busy at task-related activities, following sensible routines, and striving toward clearly understood objectives, that situations with which teachers must "cope" seldom have an opportunity to arise. Through management skills, superior teachers achieve what has commonly been labeled "preventive discipline" in the professional literature. They are not automatically superior teachers. They plan, worry, and work hard. I have never known superior teachers who "took it easy." But the secret to their success—what sets them above the good teachers who also work, plan, and worry—is their process of management. They have learned (and firmly believe) that process affects product; that how they manage their classroom significantly affects the climate, motivation, and goal achievement in their classrooms. In short, their knowledge base includes a thoughtful understanding of the importance of the Silent Curriculum [p. 145].

The achievement of affective and academic goals is an integrated and interdependent venture. No matter how affect-laden the communication used in the classroom may be, the student will not develop a positive self-concept when exposed to consistent failure experiences in the academic curriculum. The technical skills to ensure consistent demonstrations of success need to be complemented with management and communication processes that emphasize the worth and dignity of the individual. Teachers who are highly knowledgeable in the content area but deliver instruction in an arrogant manner, with no demonstrated respect for the weaker members of the class, are just as unprofessional as teachers so preoccupied with affective objectives that they fail to master the instructional skills needed to provide the consistent demonstrations of academic success that are so vital to the development of healthy self-concepts on the part of the students.

B. Knowledge Quiz: Classroom Management

Multiple Choice

Question 1   The primary goal of effective classroom management is

a.   an orderly classroom.

b.   to reduce misbehavior.

c.   to prevent misbehavior.

d.   to promote learning.

Question 2   The prevention of misbehavior is most effectively managed by

a.   reprimanding students immediately.

b.   ignoring all inappropriate behavior.

c.   maintaining strong, durable instructional procedures.

d.   keeping all desks in rows.

Question 3   A major reason for setting and implementing rules is to

a.   acquaint all students with classroom practices.

b.   restore order after an incident.

c.   demonstrate an awareness of behavior problems and a commitment to learning tasks.

d.   provide a basis for citizenship grades.

Question 4   Praise is effective when it

a.   orients students toward comparisons with others.

b.   attributes success to ability alone.

c.   is restricted to global, positive actions.

d.   uses students' prior accomplishments for describing present performance.

Question 5   Reprimands should

a.   be infrequent.

b.   be general.

c.   address specific academic errors.

d.   be given as many times as praise statements.

Question 6 Misbehavior is best approached by procedures that stress

a. replacement.
b. punishment.
c. reprimands.
d. order.

Question 7 Rules should be introduced and defined.

a. as a way of indicating respect for teacher authority.
b. as procedures that cannot be questioned.
c. as procedures that are optional.
d. as procedures that have value for individual and group functioning.

Question 8 Most interventions should be

a. quick and intrusive.
b. relatively unintrusive.
c. accompanied by a detailed explanation.
d. obvious to all students.

Question 9 The use of extreme forms of intervention should

a. cause the teacher to review present management practices.
b. show all students the teacher is serious.
c. increase a teacher's credibility with school administrators.
d. be conducted at regular intervals.

Question 10 The more you reprimand students,

a. the greater student achievement.
b. the more you need to use reprimands.
c. the greater student respect.
d. the easier it is to get attention.

Fill in the Blanks

Question 11 Reminding a student to "get back to work" would be an example of _____ _____ feedback.

Question 12 According to Brophy, attributing success to ability alone is an _____ form of praise.

Question 13 According to Brophy, attributing success to effort and ability is an _____ form of praise.

Question 14 Praise statements should _____ outnumber verbal reprimands.

Question 15 If a public reprimand is called for, address the _____ _____, not the _____, as undesirable.

Answer Key: Knowledge Quiz (Classroom Management)

Multiple Choice

Question 1   The primary goal of effective classroom management is

d. to promote learning.

Question 2   The prevention of misbehavior is most effectively managed by

c. maintaining strong, durable instructional procedures.

Question 3   A major reason for setting and implementing rules is to

c. demonstrate an awareness of behavior problems and a commitment to learning tasks.

Question 4   Praise is effective when it

d. uses students' prior accomplishments for describing present performance.

Question 5   Reprimands should

a. be infrequent.

Question 6   Misbehavior is best approached by procedures that stress

a. replacement.

Question 7   Rules should be introduced and defined

d. as procedures that have value for individual and group functioning.

Question 8   Most interventions should be

b. relatively unintrusive.

Question 9   The use of extreme forms of intervention should

a. cause the teacher to review present management practices.

Question 10   The more you reprimand students,

b. the more you need to use reprimands.

Fill in the Blanks

Question 11 Reminding a student to "get back to work" would be an example of *task engagement* feedback.

Question 12 According to Brophy, attributing success to ability alone is an *ineffective* form of praise.

Question 13 According to Brophy, attributing success to effort and ability is an *effective* form of praise.

Question 14 Praise statements should *greatly* outnumber verbal reprimands.

Question 15 If a public reprimand is called for, address the *specific action*, not the *person*, as undesirable.

C. Self-evaluation Checklist: Classroom Management

Instructions for Completing the Self-evaluation Checklist

The self-evaluation checklist on the following pages should be completed using the following scale and criteria.

1 = No change is needed in present practices.

2 = There are minor problems that can be corrected quickly and easily.

3 = There are major problems that will require a considerable investment in time and effort.

4 = I need more specific information on my own behavior before I can decide whether I have a problem.

The evaluation questions are provided as a guide to the type of specific behaviors that exemplify each of the effective teaching skills. You should feel free to add evaluation questions if you feel that such additions will increase the practicality and sensitivity of the evaluation process.

Please make supporting notes that will help describe any problems in more detail. Notes should address the context; for example, certain problems may be more or less noticeable, depending on the time, the class, the individual student, the lesson activity, and the subject being taught.

If the space provided on the evaluation checklist is not sufficient, supplement the checklist by adding descriptive material and cross-referencing supplementary material with the number of the skill and the letter of the evaluation question (e.g., Skill 2, Question c).

Additional information on the criteria and the use of the self-evaluation checklist is provided in Section C of Chapter 2.

Self-evaluation Checklist

Skill 1. Instructional Strengths
Well-planned, strong, durable procedures are used to teach the course content.

Evaluation Questions	Rating and Notes	
a. Are time management procedures, such as brisk pacing and effective transitions, used?		
b. Are functions, such as checking prerequisites and guided practice, ensuring successful student management?		
c. Are effective academic feedback and academic monitoring skills in use?		
d. Does the teacher avoid being distracted from instruction by student misbehavior?		
e. Do good preparation and planning help maintain instructional momentum?		

Skill 2. Setting and Implementing Rules
The teacher uses rules and related procedures to prevent problems and manage the classroom in a businesslike manner.

Evaluation Questions	Rating and Notes	
a. Does the teacher provide a set of rules at the beginning of the course?		
b. Do the rules specify behaviors needed for productive, instructional interactions?		
c. Does the teacher demonstrate a willingness and ability to act when rules are broken?		
d. Does the teacher establish and interpret rules to develop student support for the rules?		

Rating Scale: 1 - No change; 2 - Minor problems; 3 - Major problems; 4 - Insufficient information

Skill 3. Prevention
The teacher effectively intervenes to prevent and reduce misbehavior.

Evaluation Questions	Rating and Notes	
a. Does the teacher demonstrate increased vigilance at appropriate times?		
b. Are interventions timed to avoid disrupting the flow of the instruction?		
c. Do teacher reactions to misbehavior model appropriate social interactions?		
d. Does the teacher effectively use physical placement to monitor students and intervene effectively?		

Skill 4. Appropriate Behavior Recognized
The teacher clearly identifies and recognizes appropriate academic and classroom social interaction skills.

Evaluation Questions	Rating and Notes	
a. Are the important classroom social interaction skills clearly identified?		
b. Is teacher praise contingent, i.e., clearly linked in time and action with the student behavior?		
c. Does teacher praise leave no doubt as to who and what action is being recognized?		
d. Is teacher praise delivered in a credible manner?		

Skill 5. Limited Reprimands
Reprimands are limited in number and effectively used.

Evaluation Questions	Rating and Notes	
a. If reprimands are used, are they contingent, specific, and credible?		
b. Is there any evidence to suggest that academic errors are being equated with misbehavior?		
c. Do the tone and content of reprimands threaten student self-concepts?		
d. Are reprimands being used excessively?		
e. Do specific students receive excessive reprimands?		

D. Information Gathering: Classroom Management

This section includes two forms that may be used to gather information on classroom management. Form 6.1, "School Rules," can be used to establish rules and collect information regarding the rules and how well they are being enforced. Form 6.2, "Daily Goals," can be used to encourage students to monitor their own behavior. Directions for using the forms are included.

School Rules

Decide what rules in your classroom are necessary for maintaining a positive learning environment. Use Form 6.1b for each of your rules. (See the completed sample, Form 6.1a.) State the rule, in positive terms, in the top box. Next, write a statement explaining the rationale for the rule in the second box. (This may be helpful in providing explanations to students and parents.) Decide on the appropriate positive and negative consequences for the rule, and write a statement of the consequences under the appropriate heading.

After you have established the rules, collect daily group or individual information on how frequently the rule was broken and how consistently the consequences were enforced. Use this data to refine rules and consequences.

SCHOOL RULES

RULE # _1_ : *Raise your hand to talk.*

RATIONALE: *During formal classes, the rule is important because it saves time and prevents confusion. We can listen and learn.*

CONSEQUENCES

Positive	Negative
Verbal praise	*—Ignore students who fail to raise their hands.*

DATE	FREQUENCY OF INFRACTIONS	CONSISTENCY OF CONSEQUENCES
Monday _2/6_	Never — Constantly 1 2 3 (4) 5	Never — Constantly 1 2 (3) 4 5
Tuesday _2/7_	Never — Constantly 1 2 3 (4) 5	Never — Constantly 1 2 3 (4) 5
Wednesday _2/8_	Never — Constantly 1 2 (3) 4 5	Never — Constantly 1 2 3 (4) 5
Thursday _2/9_	Never — Constantly 1 (2) 3 4 5	Never — Constantly 1 2 3 4 (5)
Friday _2/10_	Never — Constantly 1 (2) 3 4 5	Never — Constantly 1 2 3 (4) 5

SCHOOL RULES

RULE # ___:
RATIONALE:

CONSEQUENCES

Positive	Negative

DATE	FREQUENCY OF INFRACTIONS					CONSISTENCY OF CONSEQUENCES				
Monday ___	Never				Constantly	Never				Constantly
	1	2	3	4	5	1	2	3	4	5
Tuesday ___	Never				Constantly	Never				Constantly
	1	2	3	4	5	1	2	3	4	5
Wednesday ___	Never				Constantly	Never				Constantly
	1	2	3	4	5	1	2	3	4	5
Thursday ___	Never				Constantly	Never				Constantly
	1	2	3	4	5	1	2	3	4	5
Friday ___	Never				Constantly	Never				Constantly
	1	2	3	4	5	1	2	3	4	5

Daily Goals

As needed, give each student a copy of Form 6.2, with a list of four or five individual behavioral goals written in the top box. (See the filled-in sample, Form 6.2a.) At the beginning of each day, students should select one of the goals and write it in the similarly labeled section next to the appropriate day of the week, as on the sample. At the end of the day, students should spend a few minutes evaluating their efforts to implement their selected goal, and then write comments reflecting their thoughts in the space labeled, "How well I did."

DAILY GOALS

I will try to...

1. Stay in my seat during Science class.
2. Get my homework finished in History.
3. Be friendly toward people in the lunch area.

Monday 2/6	I will try to... Stay in my seat during Science.
	How well I did: Good. I only got out 2 times.
Tuesday 2/7	I will try to... Get my homework finished in History.
	How well I did: I didn't get all of it finished.
Wednesday 2/8	I will try to... Get my homework finished in History.
	How well I did: Excellent! I finished all of it.
Thursday	I will try to...
	How well I did:
Friday	I will try to...
	How well I did:

DAILY GOALS

I will try to...

Monday	I will try to...
	How well I did:
Tuesday	I will try to...
	How well I did:
Wednesday	I will try to...
	How well I did:
Thursday	I will try to...
	How well I did:
Friday	I will try to...
	How well I did:

E. Practical Suggestions: Classroom Management

The practical suggestions in this section are based on classroom observations, experience, and a review of the effective teaching literature and teacher magazines. Feel free to incorporate any of the suggestions that work for you.

Setting and Implementing Rules

a. General Rules and Procedures.

(1) Provide explicit information about appropriate behavior.

(2) Formally teach rules and procedures so that implementation is more instruction-oriented than control-oriented.

(3) Plan when and how to teach rules and procedures. Model and practice the procedures.

(4) Predetermine consequences for appropriate behavior and inappropriate behavior. Present these consequences and the rationale for using them to your students.

(5) Review and maintain rules and procedures.

(6) Plan "wind-up" and "wind-down" activities. A good wind-up activity for the beginning of a session is a three-minute facts timing. A good wind-down activity is a large-group review session.

(7) Develop rules and procedures for different contexts, such as small groups, large groups, seatwork, transitions, and interruptions.

(8) Share your room rules with parents and ask for their support.

(9) State rules in terms of desired behaviors. Make them short and to the point. Post a copy of the rules in your classroom. Examples are included below:

Room Rules	Playground Rules
1. Stay in your seat.	1. Play with others.
2. Face forward.	2. Be a good sport.
3. Work quietly.	3. Use equipment the right way.
4. Raise your hand.	4. Follow directions.
5. Listen and work hard.	5. Come when you are called.
6. Be a good friend.	6. Use your common sense.

Sitting	Lines
1. Feet flat on floor.	1. Stand up straight.
2. Sit up straight.	2. Quiet.
3. Face forward.	3. Hands at sides.
	4. Follow the leader.
Come up when you are called.	Ask to have your work checked.

b. Administrative Rules and Procedures.

    (1) Develop a fixed seating arrangement so that attendance may be taken quickly, or have "row monitors" help with taking roll.

    (2) Review independent work daily.

    (3) Return completed papers as soon as possible.

    (4) Establish consequences for failing to complete assignments on time.

    (5) Provide procedures and space for storing students' personal belongings.

    (6) Teach students to pace themselves, using a clock.

    (7) Establish routines for assigning, checking, and collecting work.

    (8) Establish a list of activities for the first week of school, focused on matters of greatest concern to students. Make certain that the activities readily involve students and maintain a whole-group focus.

        (a) Information about teachers and classmates.

        (b) Review of daily schedule.

        (c) Description of times and practices for lunch and recess, using the bathroom, and getting a drink of water.

    (9) Establish a list of activities for new students who enter the class during the school year (see Form 6.3, "New Student Checklist").

c. Student Movement Rules and Procedures.

    (1) Place desks in a way that facilitates paths to pencil sharpener, storage area, doorway, group presentation areas, etc.

    (2) Establish rules for moving quietly about the room. Make it explicit that students walk, not run, from one area to another.

    (3) Establish consequences for appropriate and inappropriate movement in the classroom.

    (4) Control the number of students moving about the room at any one time.

d. Verbal Participation and Talk Rules and Procedures.

    (1) Make certain that students raise their hands before talking, especially in large-group situations.

    (2) After a hand raise, require that students wait to be recognized before answering questions or verbally participating.

    (3) During seatwork, students need to know when and how to get help. In addition, they need to know what to do when they finish their work. Establish procedures for these situations. Examples of activities students can do when they finish early include doing fun worksheets, listening to music using headphones, or working on a favorite puzzle.

FORM 6.3

NEW STUDENT CHECKLIST

Name _____ Grade Level _____ Date of Enrollment _____

School Previously Attended _____ City _____ State _____

Previous Teacher's Name _____

I. <u>First Day- First Week Activities</u>

_____ 1. Seating Arrangement (desk, table and chair, study carrell)

_____ 2. Introduce new student to class, principal, others.

_____ 3. Give student a tour of the building and playground area.

_____ 4. Explain basic room rules (stay in seat, hand raises)

_____ 5. Check school supplies student has brought, if any. Check these items off on supplies list.

_____ 6. Informal Testing
Describe:

_____ 7. Norm-Referenced Testing
Describe:

_____ 8. Criterion-Referenced Testing
Describe:

_____ 9. Explain policies and procedures of school, general school policies, lunchroom, bathroom, playground.

_____ 10. Assign student a buddy to guide him or her through the day.

_____ 11. Explain token economy system.

_____ 12. Independent activities--independent fun worksheets, listening to
tapes, games, art activities, other manipulatives.

_____ 13. Make sure you receive student's cumulative folder from other
school.

_____ 14. Establish student's task folders.

_____ 15. Set up student's schedule (individualized if necessary).

II. <u>Send Home with Student</u>

_____ 16. General Information form.

_____ 17. Medication policy form (if necessary).

_____ 18. School supplies list

_____ 19. Cover letter of introduction: Include school phone number,
information about lunch and milk money and any other necessary information. If possible, contact parents by phone before
student comes to school. Set up initial conference. May wish to
include a positive comment about student's first day.

Managing Interventions

    a. Arrange the Physical Environment.

        (1) Position yourself so that you can observe all students in the room.

        (2) Frequently move around the classroom so that you can observe exactly what students are doing.

        (3) Consider special seating or grouping arrangements. Arrange desks so that students are focused on what they need to work on most.

        (4) Make certain that traffic patterns are suitable.

        (5) Store materials near the area where they will be used.

    b. Observe Students.

        (1) Attend to all of the events going on at any given point in time.

        (2) Watch how groups operate, observe individual student conduct or behavior, and keep track of the pace, rhythm, and duration of classroom events. For example, two 15-minute seatwork sessions might be more appropriate for younger students than one 30-minute seatwork session.

        (3) Pick a "steering criterion group" to use as a measure of appropriate completion times. Observe the steering criterion group to decide appropriate completion times for worksheets.

    c. Communicating Awareness to Students.

        (1) Maintain eye contact with students whenever possible.

        (2) Use proximity control to let students know you are aware of what they are doing.

        (3) Engage students in questions or make comments to communicate awareness.

Increasing Appropriate Behavior

    a. Define Problematic and Appropriate Behavior.

        (1) Define problematic behaviors. For example, problematic behavior might be defined as "behavior that is serious enough to distract other members of the class."

        (2) Whenever possible, state the desired behavior. For example, if the problematic behavior is defined as "talking during seat work," also state the desired behavior as "working quietly."

        (3) Pre-define consequences for problematic behavior and inform students. Make certain that the consequences are reasonable and can be easily carried out.

       (4) Make certain you are aware of the most serious inappropriate behavior at any given time. Keep track of any potentially disruptive situations.

   b. Provide Corrective Feedback.

       (1) Provide corrective feedback immediately and consistently! Inform the student of the rule or procedure violation. It is best to state the rule violation in terms of the desired behavior. For example, don't say, "Stop running." Instead, say, "Remember to walk."

       (2) Provide corrective feedback in terms of announced consequences.

       (3) Provide corrective feedback in a quiet manner that allows students to maintain their dignity.

   c. Ignore When Appropriate (Evertson, Emmer, Sanford, & Clements, 1983)

       (1) Ignore the behavior if

          (a) The problem is momentary and is not likely to escalate.

          (b) The problem is a minor deviation.

          (c) Handling the problem would seriously interrupt the flow of the lesson.

          (d) Other students are not involved.

F. Self-improvement Plan: Classroom Management

After completing the self-evaluation checklist (Section C) and reading through the practical suggestions (Section E), you should be prepared to develop a self-improvement plan (SIP). Please complete portion A, "Classroom Management: Goals and Objectives," on the self-improvement plan, by checking the goal(s) and objective(s) you wish to include in your plan. Also, write a brief narrative describing how you plan to address the requirements in portions B–E. Complete portion F, "Results," after you have completed your self-improvement implementation project. (See Chapter 2, Section F, for a completed self-improvement plan.)

Self-improvement Plan: Classroom Management

Name _____   Class _____   Date _____

A. Classroom Management: Goals and Objectives
   1. Setting and Implementing Rules
      a. General rules and procedures.
      b. Administrative rules and procedures.
      c. Student movement rules and procedures.
      d. Other _____
   2. Managing Interventions
      a. Arrange the physical environments.
      b. Provide corrective feedback.
      c. Ignore when appropriate.
      d. Other _____

B. Practical Suggestions
   Please indicate which of the practical suggestions from Section E you plan to use to meet each of the objectives. (You may include practical suggestions from other sources as well.)

C. Specific Procedures
   Please describe the specific procedures you will use to implement the practical suggestion(s).

D. Please describe your current performance and desired performance in regard to each of the objectives you have selected. You may state the performance in terms of student behavior, such as percentage of talk outs.

E. Timelines and Change Measures
   Please describe your timelines and how you will measure change in relationship to the objective(s) you have selected.

F. Results
   Upon completion of your self-improvement project, please submit copies of this form and a brief description of the results of its implementation. Attach any raw data sheets that were used to gather information and describe any changes that were made during your project.

References

Becker, W.C. (1986). *Applied psychology for teachers: A behavioral cognitive approach.* Chicago: SRA Publishing.

Brophy, J. (1981). Teacher praise: A functional analysis. *Review of Educational Research, 51*(1), 5–32.

Crocker, R.K., & Brooker, G.M. (1986). Classroom control and student outcomes in grades 2 and 5. *American Educational Research Journal, 23*(1), 1–11.

Doyle, W. (1984). How order is achieved in classrooms: An interim report. *Journal of Curriculum Studies, 16*(3), 259–277.

_____. (1986). Classroom organization and management. In M.C. Wittrock (Ed.), *AERA handbook of research on teaching,* 3rd ed. (pp. 392–431). New York: Macmillan.

Duke, D.L. (1979). Editor's preface. In D.L. Duke (Ed.), *Classroom management* (78th Yearbook of the National Society for the Study of Education, Part 2). Chicago: University of Chicago Press.

Evertson, C.M., Emmer, E.T., Sanford, J.P., & Clements, B.S. (1983). Improving classroom management: An experiment in elementary school classrooms. *Elementary School Journal, 84*(2), 173–188.

Fisher, C.W., Berliner, D.C., Filby, N.N., Marliave, R., Cahen, L.S., & Dishaw, M.M. (1980). Teaching behaviors, academic learning time, and student achievement: An overview. In C. Denham & A. Lieberman (Eds.), *Time to learn* (pp. 1–32). Washington, D.C.: U.S. Department of Education, National Institute of Education.

Hosford, P.L. (1984). The art of applying the science of education. In P.L. Hosford (Ed.), *Using what we know about teaching* (pp. 141–161). Alexandria, Va.: Association for Supervision and Curriculum Development.

Kounin, J.S. (1983). *Classrooms: Individuals or behavior settings?* (Monographs in Teaching and Learning, No. 1.) Bloomington, Ind.: Indiana University School of Education.

Metz, M. (1978). *Classrooms and corridors.* Berkeley, Calif.: University of California Press.

Morsink C.V., Soar, R.S., Soar, R.M., & Thomas, R. (1986). Research on teaching: Opening the door to special education classrooms. *Exceptional Children, 53*(1), 32–40.

Rusnock, M., & Brandler, N. (1979, April) *Time off-task: Implications for learning.* Paper presented at the annual meeting of the American Educational Research Association, San Francisco.

Silverstein, J.M. (1979). *Individual and environmental correlates of pupil problematic and nonproblematic classroom behavior.* Unpublished doctoral dissertation, New York University.

Trenholm, S., & Rose, T. (1981). The compliant communicator: Teacher perceptions of appropriate classroom behavior. *Western Journal of Speech Communication, 45,* 13–26.

INDEX

Academic feedback, 18, 42, 54, 55, 60, 93–128, 162
  analyzing, 117–119
  concepts, 95–104
  correction procedure, 99
  data collection form, 118–119
  defined, 94
  error-prevention procedures, 99–100
  goals and objectives, 125
  and independent practice, 100–104
  information gathering, 113–119
  knowledge quiz, 105–109
  opportunities, 95–96
  practical suggestions, 120–123
  prompting, 99, 100
  psychological climates for errors, 100
  questions, 94, 96–98, 113–116
  research on, 94–104
  reactions to student responses, 98–100, 121–123, 125
  self-evaluation checklist, 110–112
  self-improvement plan, 124–126
Academic monitoring, 5, 62, 65, 102, 129–160, 162
  adaptive ability, 136–138
  concepts, 131–139
  corrective action, 133–134, 155–156, 159
  diagnosis, 131, 132
  embedded progress tests, 132–133, 136
  form, 148–150
  goals and objectives, 159
  and improvement of instruction, 134–136, 156–157, 159
  information gathering, 148–153
  instructional alignment, 136
  interaction monitoring form, 151–153
  knowledge quiz, 140–144
  mastery testing, 138–139
  practical suggestions, 154–157
  purpose of, 135
  research on, 130–139

  self-evaluation checklist, 145–147
  self-improvement plan, 158–159
  and student goals, 131–132, 154
  timeliness, 155, 159
ALT (see Time management: academic learning time)
Alter, M., 6
Automaticity, 61, 97

Becker, W.C., 169
Bergan, J.R., 6
Berliner, D.C., 6, 15, 17, 18, 19, 63, 94, 99, 102, 103, 131, 133, 166
Bickel, D.D., 6, 137
Bickel, W.E., 6, 137
Block, J.H., 64, 66
Bloom, B.S., 138
Borg, W.R., 14
Brandler, N., 165
Brooker, G.M., 163
Brophy, J.E., 14, 59, 60, 67, 94–95, 96, 97, 130, 131, 137, 167
Buchmann, M., 17

Cahen, L.S., 17, 18, 63, 94, 99, 102, 131, 133, 166
Capie, W., 3, 6
Characteristics of effective teachers, 5–6, 14–15, 19, 54, 130–131
Chase Thomas, C., 61, 66
Classroom management, 5, 20, 57, 63, 64, 67, 95, 102, 161–196
  concepts, 162–171
  daily goals form, 184–186
  defined, 162
  effective praise, 168
  goals and objectives, 194
  increasing appropriate behavior, 163, 166–167, 191–192
  information gathering, 181–186
  knowledge quiz, 173–177
  managing interventions, 164–166, 191, 194

Classroom management (continued)
  new student checklist, 189–190
  order in the classroom, 162
  practical suggestions, 187–192
  reprimands and punishments,
    167, 169–171
  research on, 162–172
  school rules form, 181–183
  self-evaluation checklist,
    178–180
  self-improvement plan, 193–194
  setting and implementing rules,
    163–164, 187–190
  task engagement feedback, 166
Clements, B.S., 192
Cohen, A., 136
Coop, R.H., 19
Copeland, W.D., 63
Cory, J., 94
Crocker, R.K., 163
Curriculum, 5, 17, 18, 20, 57, 66,
    136, 167
  "hidden" or "silent," 15, 167,
    171
  pacing, 19, 42, 46, 48

Dishaw, M.M., 17, 18, 63, 94, 99,
    102, 131, 133, 166
Doyle, P.H., 18, 20
Doyle, W., 54, 58, 162, 164
Duke, D.L., 162

Ebmeier, H., 5, 19, 65, 95, 134
Emmer, E.T., 59, 192
Evertson, C.M., 59, 192
Expectations, 66, 104, 132, 154,
    164, 166

Fairweather, J., 94
Filby, N.N., 17, 18, 19, 63, 94, 99,
    102, 131, 133, 166
Fisher, C.W., 17, 18, 63, 94, 99,
    102, 103, 131, 133, 166
Fuller, B., 6

Gagne, R., 55
Good, T.L., 5, 19, 54, 62, 65,
    94–95, 96, 97, 130, 131, 134
Gottlieb, J., 6
Grouws, D.A., 5, 19, 54, 62, 65,
    95, 134
Guided practice, 2, 5, 20, 54, 55,
    60–61, 64, 65, 66, 86–87, 89,
    96, 103, 130, 134, 136
Gump, P.S., 18, 20

Harnischfeger, A., 15
Homework, 55, 66, 84, 95, 132,
    136, 154, 155, 156

Hosford, P.L., 171
Hunter, M., 6, 55, 61

Independent practice, 2, 5, 20,
    40–42, 55, 60, 61–62, 63, 64,
    65, 66, 87, 89, 100–104, 134,
    135–136
  and academic feedback,
    100–104
  premature, 135–136
Individual differences, 64–65, 66
Individual instruction, 3, 57
Information gathering:
  academic feedback, 113–119
  academic monitoring, 148–153
  assessing engaged time, 32–37
  classroom management,
    181–186
  teaching functions, 76–83
In-service training, 8, 9

Knowledge quiz:
  academic feedback, 105–109
  academic monitoring, 140–144
  classroom management,
    173–177
  teaching functions, 68–72
  time management, 23–27
Kounin, J.S., 20, 165
Kulik, C.C., 138
Kulik, J.A., 138

Lakin, K.C., 5
Lane, S., 6
Larrivee, B., 113–114
Latham, G., 32
Lightfoot, S.L., 67

Marliave, R., 17, 18, 19, 63, 94,
    99, 102, 131, 133, 166
Medley, D.M., 3
Metz, M., 165
Misbehavior, 18, 20, 21, 43, 133,
    136, 162–163, 164–165, 167,
    169–171, 191–192 (see also
    Classroom management)
  when to ignore, 192
Morsink, C.V., 171

Needels, M., 94
Noli, P., 62

On-task behavior, 28, 32–37, 136,
    155, 165 (see also Student
    engagement)
  defined, 32
  recording, 32–33
Overlearning, 41, 61, 135
  defined, 41

Planning, 1–11, 38, 39, 65, 66
    (*see also* Self-improvement
    plan)
Practical suggestions:
    academic feedback, 120–123
    academic monitoring, 154–157
    classroom management,
        187–192
    teaching functions, 84–87
    time management, 38–44, 49
Prerequisite skills, 5, 55, 57–59,
    87, 135
Presentation of new content, 5,
    54, 59–60, 62, 63, 65, 84–86,
    89, 99, 102, 134, 135, 139
Pre-service training, 8, 9
Professionalism, 5, 7, 138, 171,
    172

Questions, 94, 96–98, 101, 102,
    113–116, 120–121
    analyzing, 113–116
    categories, 113–114
    choral responses, 97, 99–100,
        156
    clarity, 97, 120–121
    cognitive level, 97, 114
    delivering, 98, 121, 125
    diagram, 101
    difficulty, 96–97, 114, 120
    types of, 96–97, 120, 125

Research on effective teaching,
    2–6, 7, 10
    academic feedback, 94–104
    academic monitoring, 130–139
    classroom management,
        162–172
    implications of, 5–6
    teaching functions, 54–67
    time management, 14–23
Reteaching, 5, 54, 59, 60, 61, 63,
    65, 79, 96, 98, 99, 133, 139,
    156
Review, 5, 40, 55, 62, 65, 79–81,
    84, 89, 96, 97, 98, 130, 134,
    139
    daily, 55–57, 62, 79, 84, 89, 96,
        130, 134
    game, 79–81
    weekly and monthly, 55, 62, 65,
        79, 84, 89
Reynolds, M.C., 5
Romberg, T.A., 18
Rose, T., 166–167
Rosenshine, B., 6, 14–15, 54, 55,
    59, 61, 62, 96–97, 98, 99, 130,
    131
Ross, R.P., 20

Rusnock, M., 165
Russell, D., 55

Safety nets, 65, 67
Samuels, S.J., 61
Sanford, J.P., 192
Schmidt, W.H., 17
Segregation of special-needs
    students, 136–138
Self-evaluation checklist:
    academic feedback, 110–112
    academic monitoring, 145–147
    classroom management,
        178–180
    instructions for completing,
        28–29, 73, 110, 145, 178
    teaching functions, 73–75
    time management, 28–31
Self-improvement plan (SIP):
    academic feedback, 124–126
    academic monitoring, 158–159
    classroom management,
        193–194
    completed sample, 48–49
    teaching functions, 88–90
    time management, 45–49
Silverstein, J.M., 164
SIP (*see* Self-improvement
    plan)
Smith-Davis, J., 61, 66
Soar, R.M., 3, 171
Soar, R.S., 3, 171
Stallings, J.A., 15, 94
Stevens, R., 6, 54, 55, 59, 61, 62,
    96–97, 98, 99, 130
Stuck, G.B., 19
Student achievement, 18, 19, 21,
    22, 65, 94, 95, 100, 102, 104,
    131, 132, 165
Student attitudes, 59, 65, 104,
    133, 135, 136, 156, 167, 172
Student engagement, 3, 14–15,
    19, 21, 41, 55, 62, 63, 94, 98,
    99, 100, 131, 162, 167 (*see
    also* On-task behavior; Time
    management: engaged time)
Student learning experiences, 2,
    3, 4, 5, 7, 9, 54, 65, 102, 156
Student practice (*see* Guided
    practice; Independent practice)
Student success, 3, 19, 55–57, 61,
    66, 86, 87, 96, 99, 133, 136,
    156, 166, 172

Teaching functions, 53–92, 96,
    162
    analyzing instructional presen-
        tations, 76–79
    concepts, 55–62

Teaching functions *(continued)*
daily reviews, 55–57, 62, 79, 84, 89, 96
defined, 54
diagram, 56
goals and objectives, 89
guided practice, 60–61, 63, 64, 65, 66, 86, 96, 102
homework, 57, 66, 84
independent practice, 60, 61–62, 63, 64, 65, 66, 87, 89, 100–104
information gathering, 76–83
knowledge quiz, 68–72
practical suggestions, 84–87
prerequisite skills, 55, 57–59, 87
presentation of new content, 5, 54, 55, 59–60, 62, 63, 64, 65, 84–86, 89, 102
research on, 54–67
reteaching, 54, 59, 60, 63, 64, 65, 79, 96
review game, 79–81
self-evaluation checklist, 73–75
self-improvement plan, 88–90
speaking clearly and fluently, 82–83, 85, 97
summarizing, 86, 89
weekly and monthly reviews, 62, 65, 79, 84, 89
Tests, 18, 62, 65, 131, 132–133, 134, 136, 138–139, 189–190
achievement, 18, 131
diagnostic, 65
embedded, 132–133, 136
mastery, 62, 138–139
Thomas, R., 171

Time management, 13–51, 162
academic learning time (ALT), 15, 16, 18–19, 40–42, 46, 48, 58, 138–139
allocated time, 3, 15–17, 38–39, 48, 65
available time, 15
concepts, 15–22
diagram, 16
engaged time, 17–18, 32–37, 39–40, 46, 48, 138–139
goals and objectives, 46
information gathering, 32–37
instructional momentum, 20–22
knowledge quiz, 23–27
pacing, 19, 21, 42, 46, 48, 86
practical suggestions, 38–44
research on, 14–23
self-evaluation checklist, 28–31
self-improvement plan, 45–49
time-on-task, 18, 33–35
transition time, 19–20, 21, 33, 36–37, 42–44, 46, 48
Tobin, K.G., 3, 6
Transitions, 19–20, 21, 33, 36–37, 39, 42–44, 57, 64, 66, 162, 165, 187
movement during, 43, 46
routines to facilitate, 43
Trenholm, S., 166–167

Voelker Morsink, C., 61, 66

White, K.P., 19
Wiley, D.E., 15
Wyne, M.D., 19